£19.96

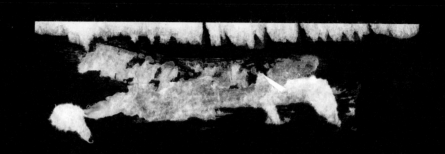

Φ

ARCHITECTURE 3s

TWENTIETH-CENTURY CLASSICS

Introduction by Beth Dunlop and Denis Hector

The architectural movements of the twentieth century have produced numerous landmark buildings of immense historical significance, and the three discussed in this anthology are prominent among them. These buildings span half a century and, in examining them, one can gain insight into the path of Modernism in the mid-twentieth century, from the early orthodoxy of the Bauhaus through to the increasingly complex forms of the Unité d'Habitation and the Salk Institute.

These three buildings – Walter Gropius' Dessau Bauhaus, the Marseilles Unité d'Habitation by Le Corbusier and Louis I. Kahn's Salk Institute – carry with them the sense of urgency and mission that Modernism sought to impart. The fact that this mission was part social and part artistic is as important, historically speaking, as the buildings themselves. Thus, to see these three buildings unfold on the following pages is also to observe the accelerating evolution of modern architecture which found, perhaps, its fullest expression – with regard to social programme and structural theory – in the work of Le Corbusier and – concerning artistic agenda – in the work of Kahn.

In all three buildings form is paramount; each is essentially a block which is interpreted for its own specific use. Yet, at the same time, in each one there is a sense of the industrial factory building – even in the Salk Institute, although the industrial form is more elusive in this case. Concrete is common to all three buildings – used both structurally and expressively, and again a historic progression becomes apparent. Certainly the Bauhaus, sheathed totally in glass, is the least aesthetically dependent on concrete. The Unité d'Habitation, however, achieves stature through Le Corbusier's powerful concrete forms – but it is in the Salk Institute that concrete is used to best effect.

The Bauhaus is, of course, the earliest of the three. In *The Master Builders* Peter Blake terms it 'one of the most extraordinary complexes of buildings to be erected anywhere in the 1920s'. It was not the first building of its kind, nor was it the only such building of its era. As Henry-Russell Hitchcock points out, however, it was the first major example of the new architecture of the time, 'illustrating on a large scale most of its possibilities and principal themes.' It was also the symbolic – and actual – home for the architects, artists, graphic designers and others dedicated to its social and artistic purpose. Significantly, it has been barred from public view – indeed from most of the non-Communist world – first by the Third Reich and the Second World War, and then because of its location in East Germany. Yet, its image remained, emblazoned in the minds of generations of architects: the concrete, glass and steel block with the outsized lettering spelling out its name – the central icon of Modernism and modern design. For many years it

was much easier to understand what the building stood for, partly because of its graphic imagery, than it was to understand the building itself. Even now, as Dennis Sharp notes on these pages, a definitive study of the building is thwarted by the paucity of printed documentation and the fact that all the drawings seem to have been destroyed.

Gropius, who came from a family of architects, designed the Bauhaus after an apprenticeship in the office of Peter Behrens. In the years just after the First World War, Germany had been racked with intellectual and social ferment, and Gropius, as an architect and designer, had been very much part of that. His early design, with his longtime partner Adolf Meyer, for the Chicago Tribune Tower (1922) presages the International Style, but his Fagus Shoe Factory – also designed with Meyer – precedes and predicts the Bauhaus. Designed and built between 1911 and 1925, the Fagus Factory bears pronounced similarities to the Bauhaus, although it relied structurally on brick rather than concrete. The fact that the art school is linked, technically and aesthetically, with a factory is germane to the whole ethos of the Modern Movement and this, in many ways, underlines the significance of the building. It is a serious, purposeful structure which was intended to reflect its mission; with its concentrated focus on educating artists and designers to produce design work for the new modern industrial age. The building embraced at once both artistry and technology and as such it had a symbolic importance that went beyond the structure itself. Reyner Banham termed it 'more a manifesto than a masterpiece', and his words are indeed apt – it is as much emblem as it is building.

'Can the real nature and significance of the New Architecture be conveyed in words?' asked Gropius in his essay entitled 'The New Architecture and the Bauhaus.' The scholar Siegfried Giedion points out, in his *Walter Gropius* that 'this multiform complex of the Bauhaus in Dessau was the first building to make a radical change with the space conception of previous centuries. Here, at one blow, the space-time conception of our period became manifest … the discerning eye can glimpse the shape of things to come.'

The building known as the Unité d'Habitation was begun in 1945 and completed in 1952 – a process that took almost seven years, given the intricacies and difficulties of postwar Europe – and it too has a symbolic importance that goes well beyond the architectural. Charles Jencks points out that, 'within architectural circles at any rate, it is one of the most famous post-war buildings in the world.' The theory underpinning the Unité is complex; indeed few architects before or since Le Corbusier have had such profound underpinnings to their work or even such grand ambitions for it.

Structurally, the Unité's roots lie in the years after the First World War, although it too is ultimately a definitive post World War II building. Early on in his career, Le Corbusier had been looking for structural solutions to the demand for mass housing, the most famous of which is the Dom-ino System (1914–15), followed by the Maison Monol (1919) and the Maison Citrohan (1921–2). This trio of prototypes provide the basic building blocks that would underlie Le Corbusier's future work: here the arched roof, the free facade and the free section emerge for the first time. More specific sources for Unité can be found in the Maison Citrohan and Le Corbusier's Immeubles Villas (1922). Its beginnings – both in terms of social intent and architecture – are also discernible at the Quartier Moderne Frugès at Pessac (1924–6). At Pessac the notion prevailed that enlightened capitalism could improve lives. Another dominant theme was the possibility of achieving a higher plane of existence through architecture and, more prosaically perhaps, the same architectural section was to be found.

The fact that the Unité was proportioned according to the Modulor (a system, of Le Corbusier's own devising, based on the dimensions of the human body) made it additionally complex and caused an interweaving of human and technological intentions. At another level, the use of reinforced concrete as a generator of form was also connected to the social purpose of the building. In an era of growing industrialism and mass production, concrete allowed architecture to achieve larger social goals.

As a product of postwar France, the construction of the Unité was constrained by the lack of available materials and because the prewar work force had been scattered and decimated. Thus, as David Jenkins writes, Le Corbusier 'explored the strengths and limitations of the material, allowing the rough wooden boards that were available for shuttering to leave fossil-like impressions of knots and grains in the concrete surface.' The rough, rusticated concrete – heavier and more aggressive than any used before the war – was indeed the product of the exigencies that controlled it. And, if Le Corbusier was less of a purist in his broad and fertile scope of thought, his handling of concrete became almost primal; it became, as Jenkins said, 'a profoundly natural material, analogous to stone and constituted literally from elements as old as earth itself.'

This, for Vincent Scully, is pivotal; in *Modern Architecture*, he wrote that the building, 'can be seen primarily in neither structural, spatial, nor abstractly massive terms – neither as a mountain, nor a cage, nor a box– but only as an articulated, unified, sculptural body. Although the individual apartment units are expressed, still, all use-scale elements, such as doors and windows, which normally make us read buildings not as sculptural creatures but as hollow containers for human activity are suppressed, so that the building, like a Greek temple with its queryperipteral colonnade, has only sculptural scale. It thus stands upon its muscular legs as an image of human uprightness and dignifies all its individual units within a single embodiment of the monumental human force which makes them possible.'

This of course is pertinent in analysing the third of the three buildings in this anthology: Kahn's Salk Institute. At the Salk

Institute, the manipulation of concrete is elevated to the status of art. Kahn was able to use it with both mechanical and artistic precision, he obsessively controlled the composition of the mix, the character of the formwork and the proportion of the grid. Steele points out that Kahn researched Roman *pozzuolana* to try to emulate the same red cast with the components of his concrete. Kahn chose to let the joints be pronounced, rather than covered or otherwise obscured, realizing that any other approach would end up with such problems as spalling. Instead he chamfered the edges and produced a now famous V-shaped groove where the edges met. Architect and historian Robert A.M. Stern called it 'one of the most perfectly constructed works in concrete ever.'

Kahn, born in Estonia but educated in the United States, was, like Le Corbusier, a complex thinker whose work stemmed from the historical, analytical, philosophical, technological and the aesthetic and he produced work that was at once compositional, structural and metaphysical. Indeed, Paul Heyer, author of *Architects on Architecture: New Directions in America*, notes the profound influence Le Corbusier had on Kahn, as much, in a way, as the Greek and Roman sites Kahn had visited in the 1920s. Scully wrote of Kahn's earlier Medical and Biology Laboratories Building at the University of Pennsylvania, noting that it 'has a challenging, rational and solemnly active reality of its own.' Kahn's buildings, said Scully, are 'reverently built, monumentally constructed of toughly jointed parts.' An apt description for the Salk Institute as well.

Charles Jencks points out that in the Salk Institute Kahn achieved a more satisfactory relationship between form, structure and space than he had in any previous project: 'In the Salk Institute project Kahn has achieved a different kind of relation between servant and served, private and public, by wrapping a circle around a square ('wrapping ruins around buildings') and by dividing the project into three types of public relation: the private living area located to the west following the slope; the semi-private area for research laboratories located at the pivotal point to the east; and the public meeting house isolated in the north west across from the private area.'

In Kahn's work there was always a profound tension between present and past, figure and abstraction. His work involved a continual stripping away to find the essence of the building or the 'Form' tempered by the circumstantial 'Design' and the infamous question, 'What does the building want to be?' Kahn himself wrote of the necessity of finding meaning in architecture, arguing that 'you don't know what the building is, really, unless you have a belief behind the building, a belief in its identity and in the way of life of man.'

The Salk Institute provided Kahn with his ideal client, the visionary medical pioneer Jonas Salk, who himself was used to asking tough, mysterious and sometimes unanswerable questions. Leland Roth quotes Kahn in *Understanding Architecture: its Elements, History and Meaning*, saying that Salk knew that 'the scientist needed more than anything the presence of the unmeasurable, which is the realm of the artist.'

The site for Salk's institute was at the edge of Pacific Ocean.

Kahn designed a full campus, but only saw the U-shaped laboratory structure built which provided research areas and private offices, and surrounded a stark courtyard paved in travertine. The courtyard owes a debt to the great Mexican architect Luis Barragán, who worked with Kahn on the design. Roth points out that 'the work spaces are expansive and functionally efficient, whereas the studies are small, intimate and private, paneled in teak, with windows angled so that the researchers look out westward toward the Pacific Ocean.' According to Stern it was a 'superbly rational structural and spatial matrix … no sentimentality, no cozy contextualism.'

Although Kahn died in 1974, Salk was still living in 1992 when the building received the prestigious 'Test of Time Award' from the American Institute of Architects, and in a statement prepared for the occasion he said, 'By creating an environment that was, in itself, a work of art, it was my hope that the Institute for Biological Studies would inspire the evocation of the art of science and that the symbiotic relationship between art and science would liberate and empower the creative forces for understanding nature and the human side of nature for improving the human condition.'

That same year, however, the Salk Institute was plunged into controversy, as it went ahead with a much-debated addition that was opposed by Kahn's family and many architectural historians, architects and scholars. The addition – which was ultimately built – was the work of two former Kahn employees at Anshen + Allen, a Los Angeles firm. The firm proposed a new main entrance and a two-wing structure to house additional offices, laboratories and an auditorium. The additional buildings were all to be 100 feet away from Kahn's building but aligned with the original terrazzo plaza and taking the place of the ceremonial grove of eucalyptus trees that had long shaped the approach to the complex. A letter by Anne Tyng, an architect, colleague and long-time mistress of Kahn, said, 'The location of the proposed addition as an "entrance" in front of the existing building and plaza gives a lesser work of architecture precedence and prominence over a masterpiece.' Nathaniel Kahn, the architect's son wrote: 'Not only will the new structures all but destroy a grove of eucalyptus trees through which visitors now enter the court, but they will also crowd the existing building so much that its singular power and beauty will be lost.' Among the architects and scholars who opposed the addition (futilely, as the addition went ahead as planned) were James Ingo Freed, Richard Meier, Robert Venturi and Vincent Scully, who wrote that the original Salk buildings 'are internationally recognized as among the greatest constructed during the Modern period.'

It is ironic that the Bauhaus and the Unité d'Habitation – both conceived and constructed as functional places, not as landmarks – should survive and even achieve the status of shrine: the Bauhaus is perhaps even more mystical because it was largely inaccessible for so long. The Salk Institute, on the other hand, was always intended to have a mystical, shrine-like presence, and, of the three, it is the one that is most reduced in stature by the imperative and will of a growing, changing world.

Walter Gropius
Bauhaus, Dessau
Dessau 1925–6

Dennis Sharp

Photography
Dennis Gilbert; cover detail
supplied by VIEW, photograph
also by Dennis Gilbert
Drawings
John Hewitt

Walter Gropius on the Bauhaus, 1926

"The Bauhaus building, commissioned by the city of Dessau, was begun in autumn 1925, completed within one year and opened in December 1926.

The building covers a ground area of 113,400 sq ft and contains approximately 250,600 sq ft of floor space. It cost 902,500 marks, or 27.8 marks per cubic m of space, including all extra expenses. Purchase of the inventory amounted to 126,200 marks. The whole complex consists of three parts. The wing of the 'Technische Lehranstalten' (technical college, later called Berufsschule) contains administration and classrooms, staff room, library, physics laboratory, model rooms, fully finished basement, raised ground-floor and two upper floors. From the first and second floor a bridge on four columns spans the roadway.

The Bauhaus administration is on the first floor and the architectural department is on the second floor of it which leads to laboratories and classrooms of the Bauhaus. The stage workshop, printing shop, dye-works, sculpture studio, packing and stock rooms, caretaker's apartment and boiler room with a coal cellar extending in front of it, are in the basement. The carpentry shop and the exhibition rooms, large foyer and adjacent auditorium with raised stage extending in front of it, are on the raised ground floor. The weaving room, the rooms for basic instruction, a large lecture hall and the connection of building to building via the bridge, are on the first floor. The wall-painting shop, metalshop and two lecture halls, which can be combined into one large exhibition hall, are on the second floor. Adjacent is the second floor of the bridge with the rooms for the architectural department and the Gropius building office.

The auditorium on the elevated ground floor of this building leads to a one-storey, intermediate wing and to the studio building, which contains the recreational facilities for the students. The stage between auditorium and dining room can be opened at both ends for performances so that the spectators can sit on either side. On festive occasions, all stage walls can be opened, thus combining dining room, stage, auditorium and foyer into one large festival hall. The kitchen with its facilities is adjacent to the dining room. A spacious terrace over-looking a large sports field is in front of the dining room.

In the five upper floors of the studio building are twenty-eight studio apartments for students of the Bauhaus, with a kitchenette on each floor. The baths, gymnasium and changing rooms and an electric laundry are in the basement.

Material and construction of the entire complex: reinforced concrete skeleton and brick walls. Reinforced slabs on structural supports, in the basement 'mushroom supports'. Steel window sashes with double weathering contacts. The flat roofs on which one can walk, are covered with welded asphalt tiles on a tortoleum-insulated base; the flat roofs on which one cannot walk, with lacquered burlap over a tortoleum-insulated base covered with concrete. Drainage through cast iron pipes inside the buildings, dispensing with sheet zinc. Exterior finish of cement plaster painted with mineral paints.

The interior decoration of the entire building was done by the wall painting workshop of the Bauhaus. The design and execution of all light fixtures by the metal workshop of the Bauhaus. The tubular steel furniture in the auditorium, dining room and studios was made according to designs by Marcel Breuer. The lettering was executed by the print shop of the Bauhaus."

Walter Gropius, *Bauhaus*, issue 1, 1926, pp.2-3 (revised translation by Dennis Sharp).

1

2

'The Bauhaus was not an institution... it was an idea', Mies van der Rohe, its last Director, said in Chicago in 1953. The institution lasted on three sites for fourteen years; the Bauhaus idea has proved indestructible.

The city of Dessau became the second official home of the Bauhaus in 1925 after 'Das Staatliche Bauhaus' had been forced to close for political reasons in Weimar. It had originally been founded in Weimar in 1919 out of the amalgamation of the existing Arts and Crafts school and the Weimar Academy of Fine Arts, with the architect Walter Gropius (1883–1969) as its Director, 1. Dessau, the capital of Anhalt in central Germany was a progressive city with expanding industries – chemical, brown coal and aircraft manufacturing (Junkers) – within its region.

The simplified title 'Bauhaus' was transferred with the institution – after considerable negotiation – to Dessau where it became a city authority-financed college. It was designated a 'High School for Design' and given university status. It was directly answerable to the Mayor and the City Council of Dessau.

When life at this enormously influential educational institution recommenced in Dessau the Bauhaus was more clearly dedicated to social ends and to the development of modern rational ideas for machine forms in art, design and architecture than in its Weimar years. The earlier Expressionistic, intuitive and rather confused German Romantic notions that had prevailed in Weimar no longer seemed relevant or applicable in the Bauhaus' new context. Times had changed. A key innovator in the Weimar school, Georg Muche later recorded that the changes he had seen at Dessau were fundamental and one of the major achievements of the Bauhaus' move. He also confessed that some of the earlier educational aims of the Bauhaus now appeared 'stupid and amateurish', not a term a German would use without considerable provocation. The economic conditions in Germany had also changed significantly in the Weimar Republic and the revaluation of the RMark in 1924 had led to new commercial expansion and confidence. The new Bauhaus built on such opportunities.

Bauhaus principles
The main principle of the 'unity between the arts' enunciated by Walter Gropius in his initial Weimar Bauhaus proclamation was still the guiding factor. It was largely adhered to at Dessau in order to underscore the newer ideas of mass production. Later, Gropius in his book *The New Architecture and The Bauhaus* (written in London in 1935) confirmed that the Bauhaus had been inaugurated with 'the specific object of realizing a modern architectonic art, which, like human nature, should be all-embracing in its scope. Within that sovereign federative

3

4

5

6

union all the different "arts" ... could be coordinated and find their appointed places'. It was a variation, of course, on the rather vague 19th century Wagnerian concept of the *Gesamtkunstwerk* or 'Total Work of Art'.[1] It was also an idea that had much in common with the ideas of the English Arts and Crafts movement that had been popularized by Hermann Muthesius. The symbolic idea of the Socialistic *Zukunftskathedrale* ('Future Cathedral') depicted by Lyonel Feininger in his famous Bauhaus proclamation cover, **2**, however, proved like a red rag to the bullish conservatives of Weimar who eventually forced the Bauhaus out of their city.

Weimar to Dessau – an uncomfortable transition

The move to Dessau from the old German city proved challenging and traumatic. It was forced on Gropius by growing political resentment in the city towards the Bauhaus and its increasingly international and 'foreign' character, **3**. The trouble came to a head in August 1923, the time of the Bauhaus' first Open Exhibition and Lecture Week. Johannes Itten had left in Easter to be replaced by the Hungarian Constructivist László Moholy-Nagy as Director of the Preliminary Course. Josef Albers, a recently graduated Bauhaus student, took up a position as his assistant. The aim of the Bauhaus week was to appeal to the world to save the institution from closure, **4**, **5**.[2]

Bauhaus week attracted an enormous number of visitors. Some estimates suggest 15,000. Although the exhibition itself and the week of special events that accompanied it were a tremendous national and international success it breached rather than healed the differences that had been developing for some time between the Bauhaus and the Weimar city authorities. The city authorities had demanded that the public should see what was going on in the Bauhaus and the exhibition, which used both Van de Velde buildings, was certainly seen as a direct initiative meeting this request, **6**. The citizens of Weimar did not like what they saw.

One of the main features of the Bauhaus Exhibition was the Haus am Horn (The House on the Horn) designed by the painter Georg Muche, **7**. A white cubic 'functional' single-storey atrium-type house unit, it was ostensibly meant to be a prototypical unit for a larger estate of houses. Now used as an unofficial archive of the Bauhaus' Weimar period it can be seen as one of the first building blocks in the new architecture of the time. It was part of a development of an earlier design by Walter Gropius for a whole estate of houses which had not proved acceptable to the student body.

Muche's model house was constructed on the edge of Weimar's famous city park in a prestigious wooded area. Unlike the craft-based timber-clad Sommerfeld Villa of

7

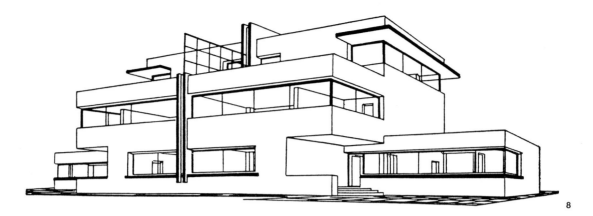

8

1920 – which had been the Bauhaus' other practical student-based product – the Haus am Horn was an early example of prefabrication with elements constructed and assembled on site (cf. Gropius' later Törten Estate house units in Dessau). Muche's project was financed by Adolf Sommerfeld, the Berlin-based contractor and timber merchant whose patronage often extended to Bauhaus experiments and designs.[3]

During the period of the exhibition Walter Gropius presented his lecture on 'Art and Technology: A New Unity' which looked forward to a progressive attitude in German industry as it moved from its craft-oriented base to the new methods of modern machine-based mass production. It was a significant contribution to the new rational thinking of the time.

Political unrest

As a new national government was elected in Berlin further unrest grew throughout the whole country and Gropius himself, known for his left wing attitudes, was investigated by the military authorities. Nothing was pinned on him. However, the Nazis gradually took over the regional government of Anhalt and the Bauhaus (which was always seen as an organization harbouring suspect figures) was soon under investigation. It was accused of neglecting German cultural values and encouraging Jewish influence

amongst its teachers and students. Furthermore, there were Bolsheviks too, under the Bauhaus beds in the form of foreign 'Masters', Kandinsky and Moholy-Nagy. Objective scrutiny soon turned into vengeful action and eventually the Bauhaus' grant was cut in half.

Simultaneously the Bauhaus staff were given suspended dismissal notices. In March 1925 it was announced that the Weimar State Bauhaus was to close. Several liberal and progressive German cities offered to take in the institution.

The offer made by the socialist democratic city of Dessau – conveniently placed mid-way between Weimar and Berlin – through the generous initiative of the city's progressive Mayor Dr Fritz Hesse (with Ludwig Grote, Director of the Dessau Art Museum) proved the most acceptable to Gropius and the 'Masters' of the Weimar school. It was agreed to move lock, stock and barrel to Dessau. This acceptance acknowledged that much greater opportunities resided in a city like Dessau with its radical political base. It was also the site of the Junkers aircraft factory, a fact that did not escape the notice of the RAF during the Second World War.

The move was also to provide Gropius with a wider role. He was to become responsible for the running and organization of the city's *Kunstgewerbeschule* and Trade School, neither of which were to be amalgamated with the

Bauhaus. Fortunately, the Mayor also believed in the Bauhaus principles and envisaged that it would aid the extension of a new kind of education related to modern ideas in the city.

It was to Gropius' great advantage that there was no building to go to. He was thus able to tailor-make a new 'Bauhaus' on the Friedrichsalle, some 2km from the city centre. Meanwhile, he opened his new architectural practice in the centre of Dessau, although without his partner Adolf Meyer with whom he had worked so closely during his early years. Meyer had opted to remain behind in Weimar. Gropius was unable to persuade the authorities in Dessau to fund a separate architecture department in the new Bauhaus so he again employed students as apprentices and assistants in his private office as he had done in Weimar. It is estimated that as many as twenty-four members of staff worked in the practice in Dessau, during the three years from 1925–28.

The Bauhaus building process

Design work on the new main building began almost immediately Gropius arrived in Dessau. It was soon approved in principle by the city authorities. The complex that emerged emphasized, in both functional and symbolic terms, Gropius' revised educational and architectural programmes. Clearly there were no longer to be any

9

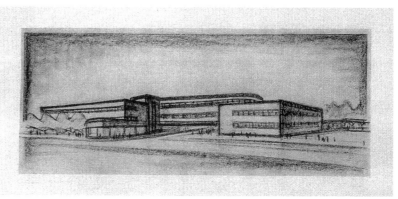

10

8 In 1923 Carl Fieger prepared a design for semi-detached houses for dentists in Dessau.
9, 10 Carl Fieger's preliminary sketches for the Dessau Bauhaus building, 1925.
11 Fieger's sketch showing the incorporation of a number of major changes, including the student *Prellerhaus*.
12 An aerial view of the Bauhaus taken at the time of construction.

12

compromises in these aims. By the middle of the summer of 1925 the drawings were complete. Work commenced on the green field site in September of that year and the new Bauhaus was inaugurated a couple of months later than had originally been planned, on 4 December 1926. Sigfried Giedion had referred to it as 'Gropius' greatest achievement'.[4] In the 1960s, Reyner Banham was to give it the status of a 'sacred site'. 'More than a manifesto, it was a masterpiece.'[5]

Scheme design

The scheme design went through a number of changes as it emerged on the drawing board. At the same time the office was also involved in the creation of three semi-detached houses for the main teachers of the Bauhaus: Klee, Kandinsky, Moholy-Nagy, Schlemmer, Schmidt and Fieger, as well as a detached house for Gropius himself. With the exception of the Director's own house (which was later destroyed in a bombing raid) the other 'double' houses remain intact today, although in need of renovation.

The cost of the new building was met directly by grants from the city of Dessau. The amount earmarked for new construction and upkeep was in the region of RMark 1 m. However, the time gap in the construction process meant that the new buildings would not be ready for a some time.

The 'Institute of Design', as the Bauhaus was now designated, was established in temporary factory and warehouse accommodation. Also, some of the 'Masters' were still living in Weimar and had to travel to Dessau to teach each week. The students – many of them almost poverty stricken – found accommodation in various parts of the town and only attended studio teaching in a sporadic way, rather like the students at the Architectural Association in London after the mid-1930s when it began to model its design studios on those of the Bauhaus.

The running of the Gropius office was now in the hands of the 25-year-old and thoroughly efficient Ernst Neufert, a former Bauhaus architecture student (1919–20) whom Gropius had employed in his Weimar atelier. Neufert was so efficient, Reginald Isaacs claims in his biography *Walter Gropius: An Illustrated Biography of the Creator of the Bauhaus*, that he was responsible for throwing out all of Gropius' early drawings and sketches, a man 'whose sense of history was subordinate to his sense of efficiency'.[6] As well as his position as the office manager for the Bauhaus jobs he also taught architecture classes at the Bauhaus. Later he was appointed head of architecture at the Bauhochschule in Weimar – Gropius' old school!

Carl Fieger, it appears, was largely responsible for making a series of preliminary sketches in 1925 that began to give a true idea of what Walter Gropius had in mind for

the new Bauhaus buildings. These drawings gave an impression of what would eventually be built on the suburban site to the south of Dessau city centre.

Fieger's early perspective drawings showed three main elements: a spacious four-storey workshop wing featuring a fully-glazed façade with pronounced mullions, a separate school wing, and a raised joint administration block which linked these two components above a roadway, **9–11**. This rather futuristic bridge spanning the roadway, the Bauhausstrasse, led to an estate area (not developed until much later) and helped to define architecturally the two main functional units of the Arts and Crafts school and the Bauhaus. A Fieger planning scheme of a year or so later linked this new road with the network that connects the Bauhaus, a sports stadium arena and the railway station.[7]

By most institutional standards the Bauhaus itself was tiny, **12**. Its size, however, belied the enormous symbolic significance it was to gain as its national and international reputation grew as an experimental and commercial laboratory for design and after 1927 (when the architecture department got underway) as a hotbed of architecture and (somewhat later) urban design. Today it is being considered as the pivotal element in the creation of a 'Future Bauhaus' proposal by the German state of Sachsen-Anhalt to house the architecture, building,

11

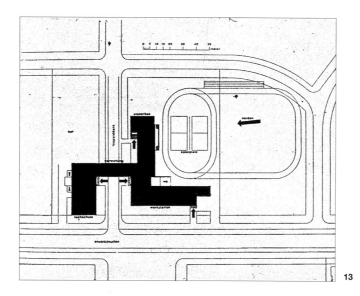

13

engineering and design facilities of a new technical university sited between the Bauhaus site and city centre.

Basic designs

Disappointingly there is little evidence available on the development of the basic architectural design ideas that lie behind the Bauhaus building itself. Nor is there much circumstantial evidence. All the drawings it appears were destroyed. Even Gropius' own otherwise definitive study of the built buildings, *Bauhausbauten Dessau* (1930), the 12th volume in the famous *Bauhausbucher* series, which he edited with Moholy-Nagy, gives little indication of the actual design process or the details of the construction. Giedion in his definitive *Walter Gropius Team and Teamwork* (1954), only provides an appraisal in summary. Furthermore, both books fail to indicate the progress of the concept through its sketch and design development stages. From more recently acquired evidence it appears that much of the preliminary design work was carried out by the students of the Bauhaus course under Carl Fieger, his chief draftsperson and detailer.[8]

Carl Fieger was born in 1893 in Mainz, the city in which he later trained as an architect before commencing work in Peter Behrens' office in Berlin, prior to joining Gropius in Weimar. Gropius worked in Behrens' office in 1907 (at the same time as Mies and Le Corbusier) where he also met his partner Adolf Meyer. Fieger went to Gropius' office in Dessau where he also acted as an architectural teacher at the Bauhaus. Interestingly he had produced a project for a pair of semi-detached houses for a site in Dessau in 1923, **8**. Recent speculation seems to support the view that Fieger was responsible with Gropius for developing the Bauhaus building's basic form and layout. The perspective drawings reinforce this view. The first, a hesitant, probative sketch indicates a complex of loosely connected buildings spread out, spatially, on the site. Service functions were to one side with access for the supply of coal to the bunkers and to the sports field. Asymmetrically placed (and it seems not to have been deviated from in any of the later designs) were the twin entrances. They faced each other across the well-defined roadway, the bridge over which clearly differentiated their separate functions. On the Bauhaus side a 'form of living' with educational, work, social and living functions grouped together, was also achieved, **13, 14**.

The brief for the new building was thus achieved by adopting a functional layout and a whole series of new disciplines. These provided it with an economical and efficient 'modern school' basis in which the title 'Master' (derived from the medieval guilds) was replaced by Professor, and the terms 'journeyman' and 'apprentice' were neatly reduced to 'student'. Lessons were renamed 'lectures' to confirm the new image of a technical college. Workshops with one director (an artist) and one instructor (a craftsman) were superseded.

A five-storey studio block with twenty-eight student bedrooms was later added to Fieger's next design and an auditorium and canteen were shown located on the first floor. This was to become the hub of the whole enterprise, an area that could be opened up in order to create a large interconnected, communal, performance and exhibition space. Work, living, eating, parties and theatrical performance were thus united in what has been called the 'miniature world of the Bauhaus'.[9]

Bauhaus interiors: colour, planes and chairs

Considerable interest was shown in the use of colour in buildings in the Bauhaus workshop courses both at Weimar and Dessau. This is perfectly understandable as much emphasis was placed in both places on the work of painters and on colour theory in the Bauhaus. This work was taken into the realm of architecture, or at least interior design, by Herbert Bayer at Weimar with his murals for the secondary staircases during the 1923 Exhibition and in the project for the Director's new office. These staircase murals have recently been fully restored.

In 1926, during the time of the construction, Hinnerk Scheper produced proposals for the exterior colouring of

14

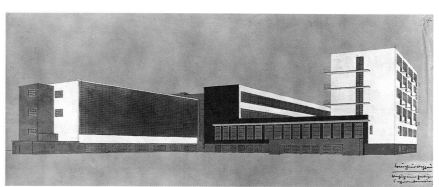

15

13 Site plan of the Bauhaus in Dessau.
14 The Bauhaus building under construction.
15 The proposed colour scheme plan was prepared by Hinnerk Scheper who was also responsible for the interior colours. In the event, the interior scheme was not used; external colours were restricted to white, black and grey.
16 Furniture and fittings were designed by Marcel Breuer and his students. Reconstructions of the contemporary light fittings were made when the building was renovated in 1976.
17 A contemporary caricature of Walter Gropius by B.F. Dolbin published in the *Magdeburger Zeitung* on 16 October 1927.
18 A contemporary cartoon by H.M. Lindhoff captioned 'Above the ruins of the house you can hear Mr Gropius moan', published in *Kladderadatsch* on 4 March 1928.

17

the main Dessau Bauhaus façades, **15**.[10] The proposed colours were dark and light grey and brown with a predominantly white finish reserved for the rendered faces of the workshop, college, administrative and student blocks. Doors were to be highlighted in process red. Most of the furniture and fittings for the new Bauhaus were designed by the newly appointed 'Professor' Marcel Breuer and his joinery workshop students. He prepared designs for use in the studios, theatre auditorium and canteen, **16**. Here, tubular steel furniture was used for the first time on a large scale. In the theatre itself he introduced chairs with steel tubular supports and seating and arm-rests made from hard-wearing, taut hessian.

The lamp fittings used in the buildings were produced by the metal workshop, most of them designed by Max Kraals and Marianne Brandt.

The signs in the building were carried out by members of the print workshop while the mural painting class was responsible for decorating many of the rooms. A contemporary report records the effect: 'the individual classrooms – and above all the library – are gently shaded in light tones. Beams are logically highlighted in specific colours. The School's dinning room works particularly well and the tripartite ceiling is picked out in red and black whilst, where there are no windows, the walls remain entirely white'.[11]

At Dessau, with all this design activity and economic self-help, it could be demonstrated that the arts and crafts had been brought together in a unified whole which emphasized the collaborative nature of the many arts connected with building.

Contemporary reactions to the appearance of the new Bauhaus were mixed, **17**, **18**. On the one hand conservative critics could slam into Gropius for his persistent use of flat roofs which Schulze-Naumburg found 'inappropriate to the German climate and customs'. While another critic, Konrad Nonn, Editor of *Zentralblatt der Bauverwaltung*, tried to prove that Gropius' use of flat roofs and glass walls were 'wholly impractical' and not 'founded on *Handwerk* as Gropius claims'. He went on: 'in the Bauhaus buildings... functional purpose is suppressed in the name of a fad in taste, and the result is the opposite of what we (i.e. *Zentralblatt der Bauverwaltung*) usually call "modern functionalism"'.[12]

Contemporary Modernist critics on the other hand, from Müller-Wulckow to Behne and the Russian writer Ilya Ehrenburg, were ecstatic. Perhaps Ehrenburg's graphic eye-witness accounts will suffice to establish the buildings' credentials:

'I approached the Bauhaus on one of the first days of spring. Delicate mists rose from the thicket of industrial chimneys; in the skies Junkers planes buzzed merrily

18

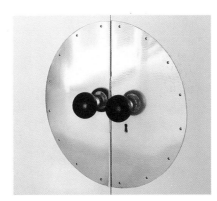

16

19 A contemporary photograph of the famous Bauhaus workshop façade.
20 An aerial view of the Bauhaus showing the development of the surroundings.
21 The glass wall played an important role in Gropius' early architecture as this section through the staircase at the Werkbund Exhibition model factory of 1914 shows.
22 As late as 1924 Gropius was still designing in the Wrightian manner. Study for the school pavilion for the Fröbel organization at Bad Liebenstein in Thuringia.
23 Perspective of Gropius' factory and offices for Kappe and Co., Alfeld-an-der-Leine, 1924.
24 Study for the design of the International Academy by Gropius in Erlangen, 1924.
25 The industrial city of Kharkov which Reyner Banham compared with the Dessau Bauhaus.

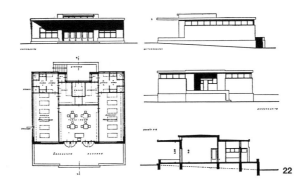

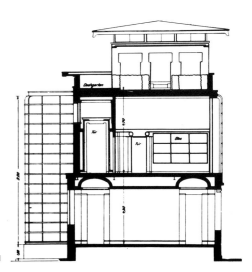

about, and there was a smell of March in the air and of smoke and chalk. When I finally saw the Bauhaus which seems to be cast of one piece like a persistent thought, and its glass walls which form a transparent angle, united with the air and yet separated from it by a distinct will – I stopped instinctively. It wasn't surprise in the face of a sensible invention, no – it was simply admiration'.[13]

There are numerous other epistles of ecstasy recorded on seeing the manifestations of a new architecture in Dessau in 1926, **19**.[14]

There really was no other building in Europe quite like Gropius' Bauhaus, **20**. It was, Banham has written, 'the first unmistakable harbinger of an international style'.[15] The stuttering Wright derived that Modernism, seen in Gropius' pre-war factories at Alfeld-an-der-Leine and at Cologne was replaced by an articulate and somewhat complex language of simple cubic forms, transparent surfaces and elegant internal spaces, **21**. The transitional period, when Gropius and Adolf Meyer were practicing, saw a deliberate change towards the simplification of the architectural object. Nothing in contemporary German architecture would ever be the same again. Followed by the international demonstration of Modernist tendencies a year later in Stuttgart on the Weissenhof the Bauhaus has a special place in the development of modern architectural principles. Having moved away from Wrightian precepts, **22** (borrowed from the pages of the famous Wasmuth publications) and a short Expressionist phrase, Gropius moved with his partner (and former colleague from the Behrens office) Adolf Meyer, towards the rationalistic *Sachlichkeit*. In schemes such as the *Chicago Tribune* Tower competition entry, the Kappe Factory, Alfeld-an-der-Leine, **23**, the Auerbach House at Jena and principally the International Philosophical Academy for Erlangen (1924), **24**, an anticipation or foreshadowing of the Bauhaus buildings' main characteristics can be observed. Gropius' design reflected above all the mood of the times towards internationalism, as well as to the reduction of formal elements in design. Like De Stijl painting, in a sense, the Bauhaus was composed of basically related functional elements that produced a cohesive interrelated asymmetrical whole. As Banham wrote in his *Theory and Design in the First Machine Age*, 'The planning is ...like nothing else of the period in its centrifugal organization... Equally new and rare is the mode of vision – the emphasis in (the book) *Bauhausbauten Dessau* is the first and foremost on a set of air views of the buildings... The three-dimensional quality of the planning is also remarkable, with two storeys of the school bridged across the road...' and here Banham compares the Russian Constructivist work at Kharkov, **25**.[16]

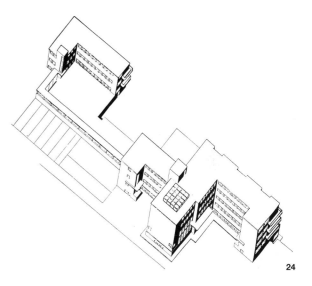

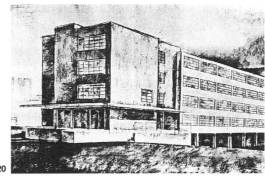

Ehrenburg felt the Bauhaus said something about 'the triumph of clarity'. He wrote, 'for the first time the earth sees here a cult of naked reason... every angle, every line, each of the smallest details repeats insistently the closing words of theorems, forgotten since schooldays: "what was to be proven"'.[17]

Compositional elements: corporeality

With the new Bauhaus building Gropius underlined the notion of the building as a 'total work' of compositional architecture. It was a clear articulation of built form that possessed none of the simple-minded functionalism of other contemporary modern structures. Early as it was, it appeared as a mature example of the *neues Bauen* which was no longer dependent on the Wrightian references that had been associated with Gropius' earlier pre-war work. In its report of the opening of the Bauhaus in Dessau, a 1926 issue of *Kunst and Künstler* underlined this architectural maturity:

'The new buildings for the Academy and workshops can indeed be recognized as a model of today's architectural achievements. The consistent exploitation of the potential of the new materials and methods has enabled the problems posed by a major project to be solved in exemplary fashion. The plan of the building, which consists of three individual but intimately connected parts has been most carefully thought out, and functional requirements are met within a whole which, in the disposition of space alone, creates an impressive effect'.[18]

Describing this intimate connection and the layout of the buildings' compositional elements, Walter Gropius compared the complexities of its design to aspects of historical architecture. 'The typical building of the Renaissance or the Baroque has a symmetrical façade, an approach leading up to its central axis... .' He claimed, furthermore, that it eschewed classical models. 'A building produced in the spirit of our times rejects the imposing model of the symmetrical façade. You have to walk right round the whole building in order to appreciate its corporeality and the function of its various parts'[19], **26**.

Besides the functional and windmill-shaped plan, what caught most commentators' imagination was the appearance of the outside of the workshop building as a see-through glazed block, **27**. Transparency was no longer simply an illusion – it could be seen here as a practical effect. It gave the building a dramatic quality creating an effect that Arthur Korn later said gave the feeling that it was '*Da und nicht Da*' – 'there and yet not there'.

The huge curtain window wrapped itself around the corner and receded back to the main Bauhaus entrance. It emphasized the 'mechanical' and the open spatial nature of the new architecture. Internally, the workshop spaces were flooded with light. Inevitably this caused internal over-heating on sunny days. At night the exterior lit up like an illuminated box providing a mature example of the new German '*Lichtarchitektur*'. There was as much window as wall on the workshop façade of this building. The load-bearing columns were (as Le Corbusier demanded) recessed back from the main walls and the whole of the workshop building could be viewed as a huge expanse of industrial glass windows. This, the predominant element in the design, was carefully linked in one direction by a two-storey administrative bridge. The student studio/bedroom accommodation of the *Prellerhaus*[20] which lay on the far side of the site overlooked portly villas and the wooded areas of Dessau.

The composition of Gropius' building could be appreciated at the time as a complete object in the landscape rather than as it is today, as part of an expanded city. The compositional idea was simply expressed. The main road frontage with its simple flat roofs was a three-storey horizontal shape poised over a recessed but half-exposed basement. Its horizontality was in direct contrast to the single vertical feature, the rear student block. On the south corner of the workshop block large letters, BAUHAUS, explained the new building's purpose.

26 'You have to walk right round the whole building in order to appreciate its corporeality and the function of its various parts' wrote Walter Gropius. This sequence of photographs goes around the Bauhaus in an anti-clockwise fashion.
27 A view looking from the administrative wing towards the workshop block.

27

28

28 The 'free-standing' glazed workshop wall with the line of radiators behind.

29, 30 Many types of opening lights were introduced from the Fenestra-Crittall range, from the hopper to the mechanically-operated 'range' of windows.

31 A night-time shot looking across the administrative bridge façade.

29

30

31

Bauhaus construction

The construction of the building was conventionally modern with an in-situ reinforced-concrete skeletal framework, with the columns exposed on the inside of the building, **28**. The infill brick walls were rendered on the outside to receive the white painted finish. Reinforced hollow clay tile floors were supported on beams running between the columns. At basement level a sturdier structural concrete mushroom column head was introduced. The flat roofs were covered with a new proprietary roofing material (which failed disastrously some years later) while the roof to the student block was covered with concrete slabs and designed as an external roof terrace. Universal section steel windows were used throughout with double-weather contacts and plate glass, **29, 30**. These were similar in pattern to the windows used earlier in Alfeld-an-der-Leine's *Faguswerke* administrative block.

Functional layout

The workshop block at basement level contained the stage, printing and sculpture workshops as well as ancillary rooms for dyeing and storage. It also housed the heating services and the boilers which were fuelled by local brown coal. The ground-floor plan provided for a joinery workshop with large display rooms before it

32

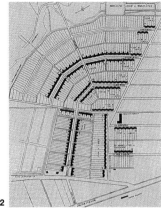

35

merged into the studio wing with its auditorium. The weaving workshops and preliminary course classrooms were situated on the second floor while the administrative offices extended on the lower floor of the bridge that led to the technical school. Situated on the second floor were the metalwork and wall painting workshops. This level also incorporated the two expandable lecture rooms adjacent to the upper floor of the bridge in which Gropius' architectural practice was housed. Later the architecture department, under the Swiss, Hannes Meyer, occupied this whole bridge wing, **31**. The so-called 'Technical School' wing contained most of the other administrative offices and staff rooms as well as the model-making workshops and library.

The key social elements in the whole design were the theatre auditorium and the canteen which were situated in the single-storey section that connected the workshop block with the student wing. The kitchens that supplied the canteen were located on the ground floor of the student block under which were the gymnasium plus additional storage space.

The five-storey studio block itself contained twenty-eight apartments and provided students with a shared kitchen on each floor. Sixteen of the apartments had projecting balconies facing east which were popular points for student *poseurs* and artists who performed

when parties and festivities took place in the buildings or when home-movies were being made.

Bauhaus revival

In 1976, at the time of the 50th anniversary of its opening, the Bauhaus was fully restored by the German Democratic Republic, **37**. The conservation office of the Dessau City Architect's Department was responsible for the work itself. A considerable amount of finance and conservation expertise was put into the restoration and this has proved sufficient to enable it to withstand the vagaries of the local climate and use over the past seventeen years. More recently, additional renovation work has been carried out and on the whole it is still in remarkably good condition. However, the steel workshop windows originally manufactured by Fenestra-Crittall with their universal steel sections, were carefully replaced by new extruded section aluminium ones. These remain in good working order. The canteen still operates successfully for staff, students and visitors and the famous cubic-shaped auditorium has been carefully re-furnished with copies of the Breuer steel and hessian-linked chairs, **38**, **39**.

Professorial houses

Having suffered from decades of neglect the professors' houses are still in a distressed condition, **33**, **34**. A year or

so ago rendered surfaces had spalled and render had peeled away; the original plain brickwork was exposed in places; broken windows and the unkempt landscaped surroundings showed the extent of years of neglect. The villa designed for and occupied by Gropius and his wife had also formed part of this group of houses before it was bombed during the war. Now only the basement and part of the garage remain. The original house has been replaced by a squarish pitched-roofed bungalow.

The six units on the site (the three *Döppelhauser*) are important examples of the architectural language of the mid-1920s with their new cubic, clear-cut functional forms. Their construction had begun in the summer of 1925 and like the Bauhaus they were rendered and had troublesome flat roofs. Each was designed by Gropius as a generous spacious, individual unit incorporating internal studios, living and bedroom accommodation. Most of them had external roof terraces. It is said that Gropius never refused to carry out any of the numerous last minute alterations demanded by the professors' wives.

Gropius' success at Dessau was confirmed by a number of commissions by the city authorities. Some buildings in the Dessau area not related directly to the Bauhaus were designed in Gropius' architectural office, for example the Labour Exchange in the city centre, **36**; a highly original single-storey top-lit building with semi-

33

34

32 Prefabricated housing units with an original, unaltered façade on the left.

33, 34 The Masters' houses in a nearby wooded area in Dessau, still in urgent need of renovation.

35 General plan of the Törten Estate, Dessau, 1926–30.

36 Walter Gropius' Labour Exchange, Dessau, 1929.

37 The original studio layout in the architecture section.

38, 39 The workshop block has many uses today, laid out (left) as studio space and (right) as an exhibition hall.

36

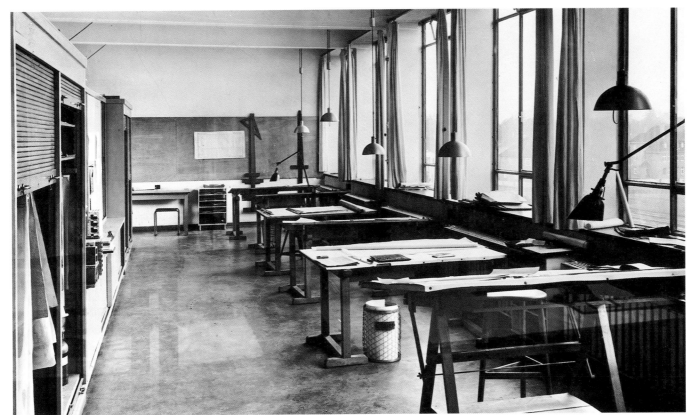

37

38

39

circular plan, and the first stage of an experimental estate of workers' standard house units which grew in three phases from 1926–30, **32**, **35**.

The cooperative store and flats of the *Konsumverein* of 1928 – one of Gropius' last Dessau designs – provided the central feature for the Törten Estate, **40**. Today, it still plays an important role on the estate as a shop, community centre and café, but like its surrounding houses is also in urgent need of refurbishment. All the single-house units on the estate have been altered and extended bar one which is a token symbol to Gropius' original interiors.

One of the more controversial buildings erected in Dessau Törten was an experimental 'steel house' designed by the Bauhaus weaving workshop Master, Georg Muche, in conjunction with Richard Paulick (who was later to run Gropius' architectural office in Berlin), **41**. It contributed – as a practical exemplar – to the lively discussions on standardization going on at the time in the Bauhaus itself with Hannes Meyer and others. Gropius was not at all happy with the design although a year later at Stuttgart he developed a similar prefabricated structure on the Weissenhof. Restored in 1976 it is undergoing refurbishment again and will soon be closely linked to the Bauhaus. The original design was based on the use of prefabricated steel sheet metal panels and column supports. It was site-assembled on a concrete foundation.

Muche's steel house had a history. He recalled in the *Bauhaus Journal* (1927) that its design ideas went back to the time he was experimenting with the Haus am Horn erected at the Weimar Bauhaus Exhibition in 1923. It was designed as a single-storey, flexible and extensible family unit. But, at the time Muche confessed, 'all types of steel constructions for houses are still primitive'. Also it needed far too much steel, a point that was rectified by Gropius' more economical housing in Stuttgart in 1927.

Near the steel house, and on the same edge of the Törten Estate, Carl Fieger designed his own very individualistic family house in 1927, **42**. The two-storey rendered house, which has suffered from neglect and an unsympathetic extension, incorporated a fine curved staircase tower that led up to a narrow bedroom wing forming one side of the L-shaped design. The re-entrant thus formed was filled by the living room. The roof of this living room served as a sun terrace to the bedrooms.

One of the most reassuring aspects of the revival of the Bauhaus is that it symbolizes the strength and purposes of Modern architecture, art and design. The Dessau Bauhaus and its predecessor at Weimar are today seeking a new identity which, once the traumatic conditions of reunification are resolved and new aims established, will again focus attention on the original venues. In *Idee und Aufbau* Gropius wrote about the way he saw the Bauhaus:

'Its responsibility is to educate men and women to understand the world they live in and to invent and create forms symbolizing that world'.[21] That was 1923. In 1935 whilst in London he enlarged on his ideas: 'Our ambition was to arouse the creative artist from his other worldliness and reintegrate him into the workaday world of realities: and at the same time to broaden and humanize the rigid almost exclusive material mind of the businessman. Thus our informing conception of the basic unity of all design in relation to life was in diametrical opposition to that of "art for art's sake" and to the even more dangerous philosophy it sprang from: business as an end in itself'.[22]

The pertinency of such views is clearly still with us. They reflect a current problem as architecture emerges out of a difficult and by all accounts posthumous phase of anti-Modernism. Who would now believe there is any relevance for example in Tom Wolfe's contention that Gropius' aim was after all only a loony battle over the lost bourgeoisie.[23] As we move today into the arena of 'Design Build' in which the new business managers (unnumbered and mainly untrained and unfailingly incompetent and unschooled in matters architectural) take over the role of designer in order to fit a preordained budget in a undeveloped design, it becomes obvious that a unique experiment like that of Gropius' Bauhaus has much more than passing historical significance.

40 The *Konsumverein*, a seven-storey apartment block and community information centre.
41 George Muche's steel house at Dessau Törten was renovated in 1976 but has since been neglected as this picture taken in 1990 indicates.
42 Carl Fieger's own house, Dessau Törten.

Notes

1 Walter Gropius, *The New Architecture and the Bauhaus*, London, 1935. Trans. P. Morton Shand.
2 See S. Giedion, 'Bauhaus, v Bauhaus woche zu Weimar', *Das Werk*, Vol X, 1923.
3 See G. Muche, *Ein Versuchshaus des Bauhaus*, Weimar, 1923.
4 S. Giedion, *Walter Gropius*, London, 1954, p.43.
5 R. Banham, *Guide to Modern Architecture*, London, 1962, p.148.
6 R. Isaacs, *Walter Gropius*, Boston, 1991, p.126.
7 See plan in C. Engelmann and C. Shädlich, *Die Bauhausbauten in Dessau*, Berlin, 1991, p.21.
8 See for example, Isaacs, op. cit., pp.72 and 151 and Engelmann and Shädlich, op. cit. The latter shows the development of Fieger's sketch schemes.
9 A vivid account of life in the Bauhaus at Dessau is given by T. Lux Feininger in *Bauhaus and Bauhaus People*, New York, 1970, pp.173–94.
10 For a review of Scheper's colour work see H. Dearstyne and D. Spaeth (ed.), *Inside the Bauhaus*, London, 1986, pp.148–9.
11 See M. Droste, *Bauhaus 1919–33*, Berlin, 1990, p.123.
12 B. Miller Lane, *Architecture and Politics in Germany 1918–45*, Cambridge, Mass., 1968, pp.134–5.
13 From an article in the *Frankfurter Zeitung*, 1926.
14 However, the penetration of those ideas in England was slow and faltering. Although not initially affected by the growing premonition of war that obscured later German developments in the arts from the British gaze after 1932 nothing will be found on the Dessau Bauhaus, for example, in the annals of the AA or RIBA until well into the 1930s.
15 Banham, op. cit., p.287.
16 Banham, op. cit., p.287.
17 From an article in the *Frankfurter Zeitung*, 1926.
18 Quoted in S. Giedion, *Space, Time and Architecture*, 4th edn, London, 1941.
19 Gropius *idem*, p.58.
20 Named after the earlier student atelier at Weimar.
21 From W. Gropius, *The Scope of Total Architecture*, London, 1956, p.23.
22 Gropius, op. cit., p.24.
23 Tom Wolfe, *From Bauhaus to Our House*, London, 1982, pp.10–13.

Chronology

March 1919
Opening of 'Das Staatliche Bauhaus' in Weimar
September 1925
Bauhaus closes in Weimar Commission for the new Bauhaus to be combined with the Dessau Technical College
4 December 1926
Bauhaus opens in Dessau
1926
Masters' houses constructed
1 October 1932
Dessau Bauhaus closes and staff and students moved to Berlin-Steglitz. It was later taken over as a Nazi training school
11 April 1933
The Bauhaus in Berlin is finally closed by the Nazis
1976
The Bauhaus is refurbished by the German Democratic Republic and reopened as 'The Bauhaus, Dessau'

Bibliography

Comprehensive bibliographies on Walter Gropius and the Bauhaus can be found in a number of major primary sources including:

The American Association of Architectural Bibliographers, *Walter Gropius: A Bibliography Part 1*, Vol 1, 1965, pp.23–43. This was followed by Vol 111, *Walter Gropius*, 1966.
Sharp, Dennis, *Sources of Modern Architecture, A Critical Bibliography: Walter Gropius*, London, 1981, pp.53–4.
Wingler, H.M., *The Bauhaus: Weimar Dessau Berlin Chicago*, Cambridge, Mass., 1969, pp.627–47.

Publications concerned with the Dessau Bauhaus buildings, their decoration & furnishing include:
Bauhaus Kolloquium Weimar 1979, Hochschule für Architektur und Bauwesen, Part 4/5, 1979 (a special publication devoted to the development of the Bauhaus and its relationship to other educational centres in Germany during the 1920s and 1930s).
Bayer, H., Gropius W. and I., *Bauhaus 1919–1928*, New York, 1938, 2nd printing Boston, 1952.
Bayer, H. et al., *50 Years Bauhaus*, catalogue of the exhibition at the Royal Academy of Arts, London, 1968.
Dearstyne, Howard, (ed. David Spaeth) *Inside the Bauhaus*, London, 1986.
Engelmann, Christine and Schädlich, Christian, *Die Bauhaus Bauten in Dessau*, Berlin, 1991.
Giedion, S., *Walter Gropius: Work and Teamwork*, London, 1954.
Gropius, Walter, *Bauhausbauten Dessau*, Bauhaus Book No. 12, Munich, 1930.
Gropius, Walter, *The New Architecture and The Bauhaus*, London, 1935 (trans. P. Morton Shand; intro by Frank Pick).
Gropius, Walter, *The Scope of Total Architecture*, London, 1956.
Isaacs, Reginald, *Walter Gropius*, Boston, 1991. (See also Professor Isaacs' article 'The Bauhaus' in **Wilkes, J.** (ed.) *Encyclopedia of Architecture: Design, Engineering and Construction*, Vol 1, New York, 1988, pp.414–21.)
Neumann, Eckhard, *Bauhaus and Bauhaus People*, New York, 1970.
Wingler, H.M., *The Bauhaus: Weimar Dessau Berlin Chicago*, Cambridge, Mass., 1969, p.627.

Bauhaus publications

Originally published as a series by Albert Langen Verlag, Munich, 1925–30. Reissued by Florian Kupferberg Verlag, Mainz, 1965–
Gropius, W., *Internationale Architektur*, 1925 (2nd edn 1927).
Klee, P., *Pädagogisches Skizzenbuch*, 1925 (2nd edn 1928). English trans. *Pedagogical Sketchbook*, London, New York, 1944.
Meyer, A. (ed.) *Ein Versuchshaus des Bauhauses in Weimar*, 1925.
Schlemmer, O., *Die Bühne im Bauhaus*, 1925. English trans. *The Theater of the Bauhaus*, Middletown, Conn., 1963.
Mondrian, P., *Neue Gestaltung*, 1925.
Van Doesburg, T., *Grundbegriffe der neuen gestaltenden Kunst*, 1925. English version *Principles of Neo-Plastic Art*, London, Greenwich, Conn., 1969.
Gropius, W. (ed.) *Neue Arbeiten der Bauhauswerkstätten*, 1925.
Moholy-Nagy, L., *Malerei, Photographie, Film*, 1925. (2nd edn *Malerei, Fotografie, Film*, 1927.) English version *Painting, Photography, Film*, London, Cambridge, Mass., 1969. (Reprinted Cambridge, Mass., 1973.)
Kandinsky, W., *Punkt und Linie zu Fläche, Beitrag zur Analyse der malerischen Elemente*, 1926 (2nd edn 1928). English trans. *Point and Line to Plane*, New York, 1947.
Oud, J.J.P., *Holländische Architektur*, 1926 (2nd edn 1929).
Malevich, K., *Die gegenstandlose Welt*, 1927. English trans. *The Non-Objective World*, Chicago, 1959.
Gropius, W., *Bauhausbauten, Dessau*, 1930.
Gleizes, A., *Kubismus*, 1928. Trilingual edn *And Cubism*, Basel, 1962.
Moholy-Nagy, L., *Von Material zu Architektur*, 1929. English trans. *The New Vision from Material to Architecture*, New York, 1930.

Photographs

Previous pages, the main
elevation of the Dessau Bauhaus
with its great transparent glazed
workshop block.
Left, the Technical College
is seen here to the left, with
the workshop block beyond.
Right, the two entrances
to the Technical College and
the Bauhaus itself lay between
the solid and transparent
façades of the new building.

FACHHOCHSCHULE ANHALT

Previous pages, banks
of opening sashes were
coupled together on the
workshop block façade.
Above and right, the linked
ranks of opening lights were
controlled by a chain and pulley
system that retained open
windows at an equal distance.

Far left, the Bauhaus entrance.
Left, the view towards the
Technical College entrance.

The student *Prellerhaus* is seen here to the left with the administrative block bridge on the right.

The *Prellerhaus* balconies caused controversy among architects, because they were seen to be too decorative.

Previous pages, the celebrated
sub-dividing roadway between
the Technical College at the
Bauhaus originally led nowhere.
Today, it provides a pedestrian
route through the complex.
Above, the Bauhaus staircase
used as part of a bent-metal
chair exhibition in the building.
Right, the corridor side of the
administrative bridge.

The reinforced concrete
structure with its shaped profile
is seen here, far left, from inside
a studio workshop; left, corner
detail and above, the junction of
the structure and curtain wall.

The administrative offices
on the bridge have recently
been transformed by a new
colour scheme.

At the time of the 1976
refurbishment, light fittings
and door furniture were renewed
throughout the building.

The sombre external
appearance of the Bauhaus
today is much enlivened by
the glimpses of internal colour,
seen particularly after dark.

Site plan

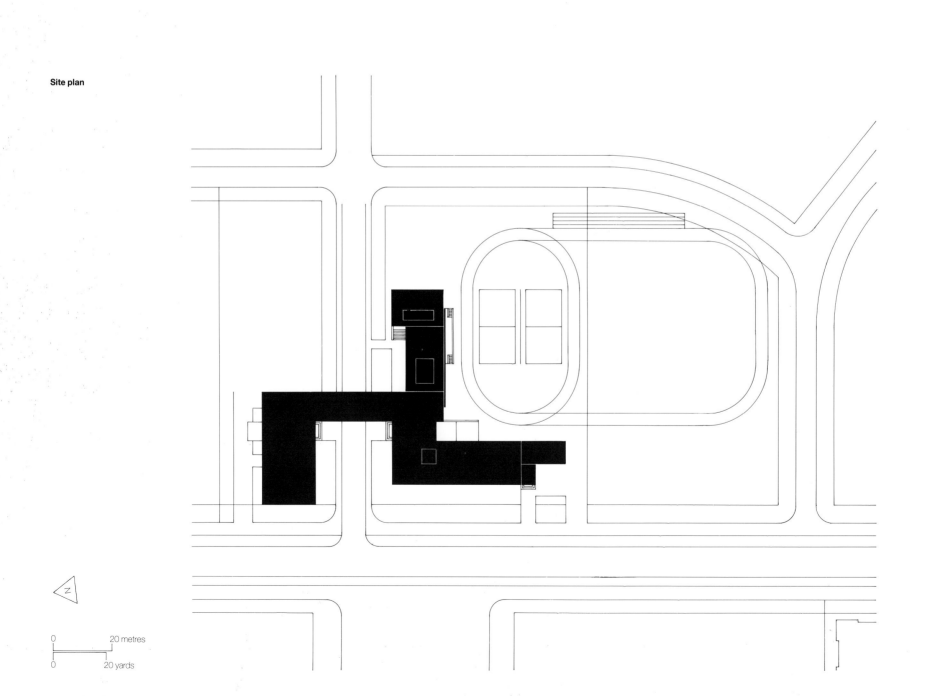

N

0   20 metres

0   20 yards

Location plan

1 Bauhaus building
2 master's house
3 Dessau Törten Estate
4 *Konsumverein*
5 Muche's steel house
6 Fieger's house
7 balcony houses
8 labour exchange
9 Kornhaus by Fieger
10 main railway station
11 Dessau-south station
12 town hall

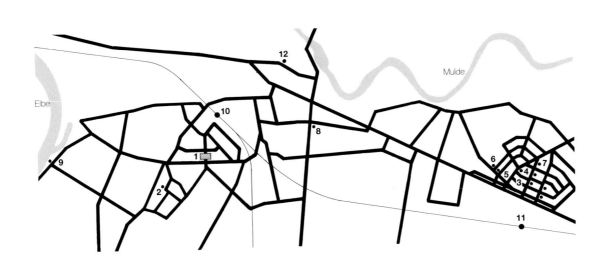

Basement plan

1 baths, gymnasium,
changing rooms, laundry

2 stage workshop, printing
shop, dye-works, sculpture
studio, packing and stock
rooms, caretaker's
apartment, boiler room/
coal cellar

3 laboratories, classrooms

(the exact layout is not known)

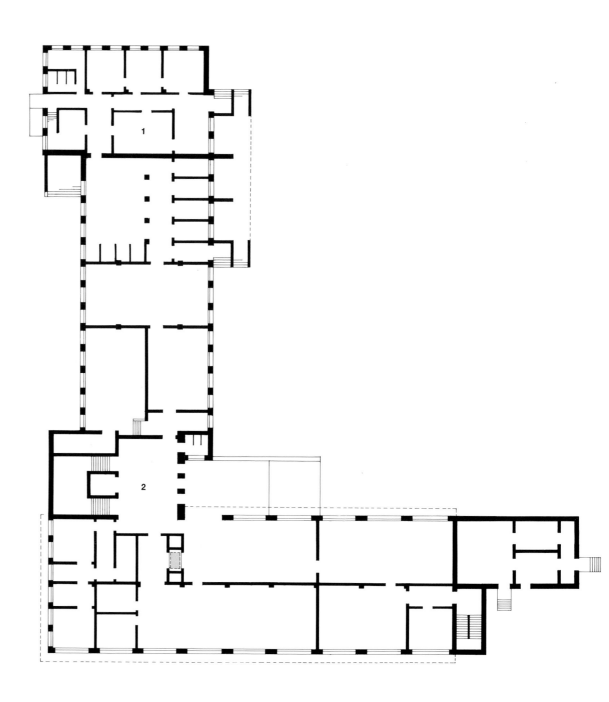

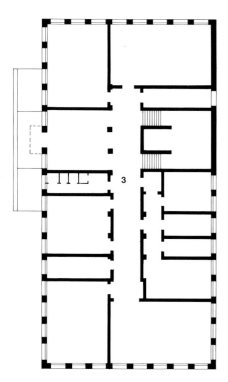

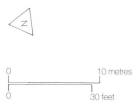

0   10 metres

0   30 feet

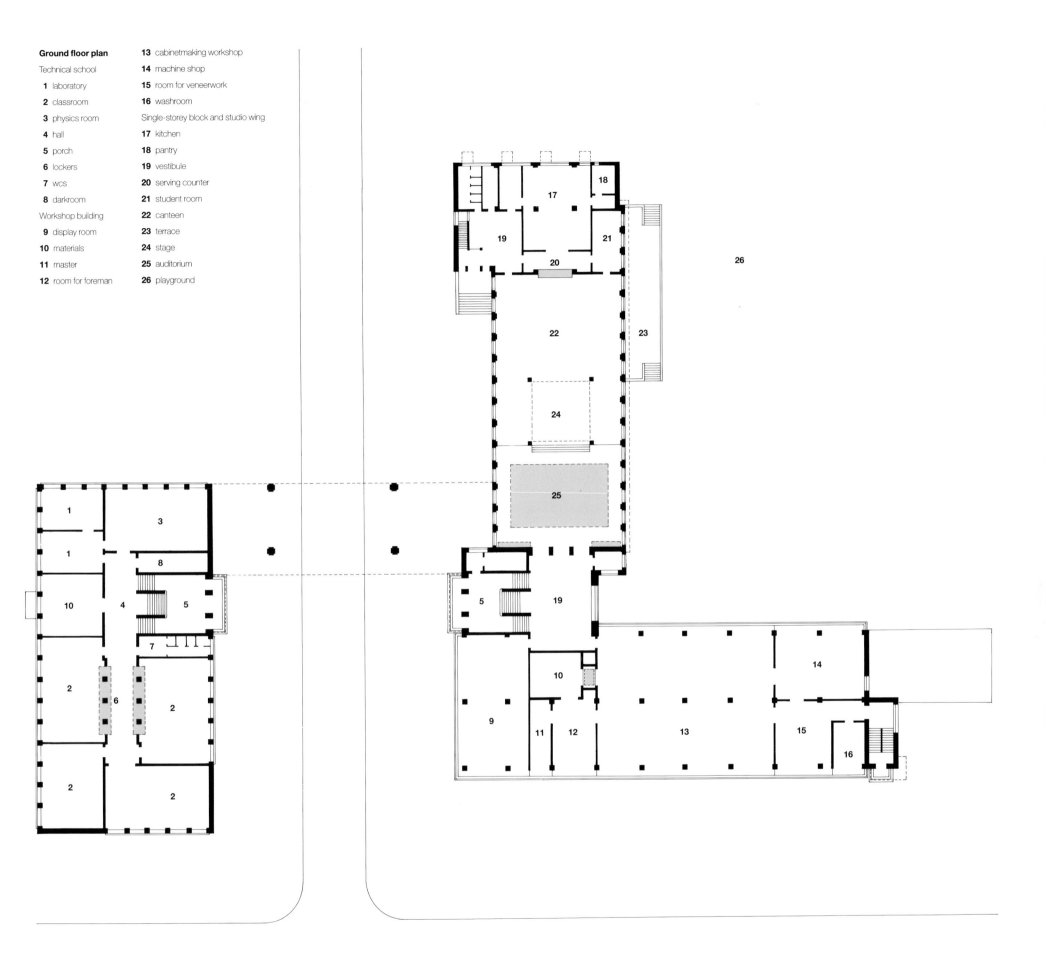

Ground floor plan

Technical school

1 laboratory
2 classroom
3 physics room
4 hall
5 porch
6 lockers
7 wcs
8 darkroom

Workshop building

9 display room
10 materials
11 master
12 room for foreman

13 cabinetmaking workshop
14 machine shop
15 room for veneerwork
16 washroom

Single-storey block and studio wing

17 kitchen
18 pantry
19 vestibule
20 serving counter
21 student room
22 canteen
23 terrace
24 stage
25 auditorium
26 playground

First floor plan

Bridge (administration building)

1 hall
2 library
3 typing
4 waiting room
  (technical school)
5 administration
6 conference room
7 director
8 Bauhaus administration
9 book-keeping (accounting)
10 cashier
11 Bauhaus waiting room
12 telephone

13 lecture room

Technical School

14 staff room
15 vestibule
16 classroom
17 lockers
18 materials
19 workshop for prelim. course
20 weaving workshop
21 master
22 wardrobe
23 washroom

Studio wing

24 wcs
25 studio

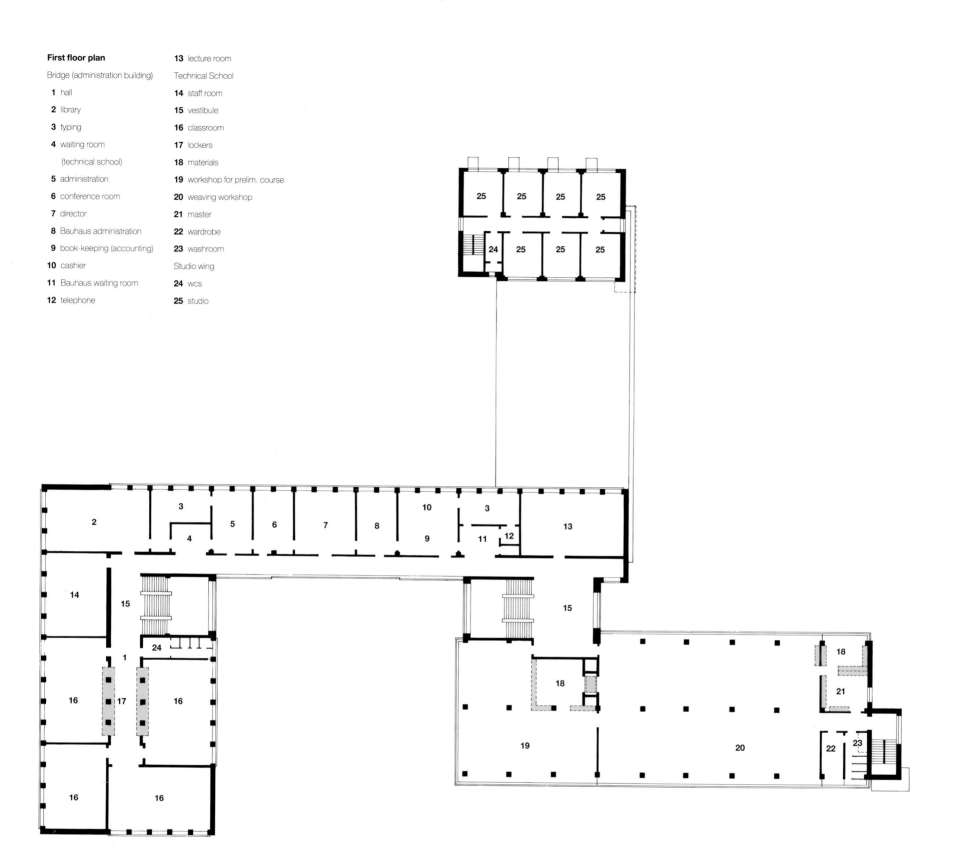

0   10 metres

0   30 feet

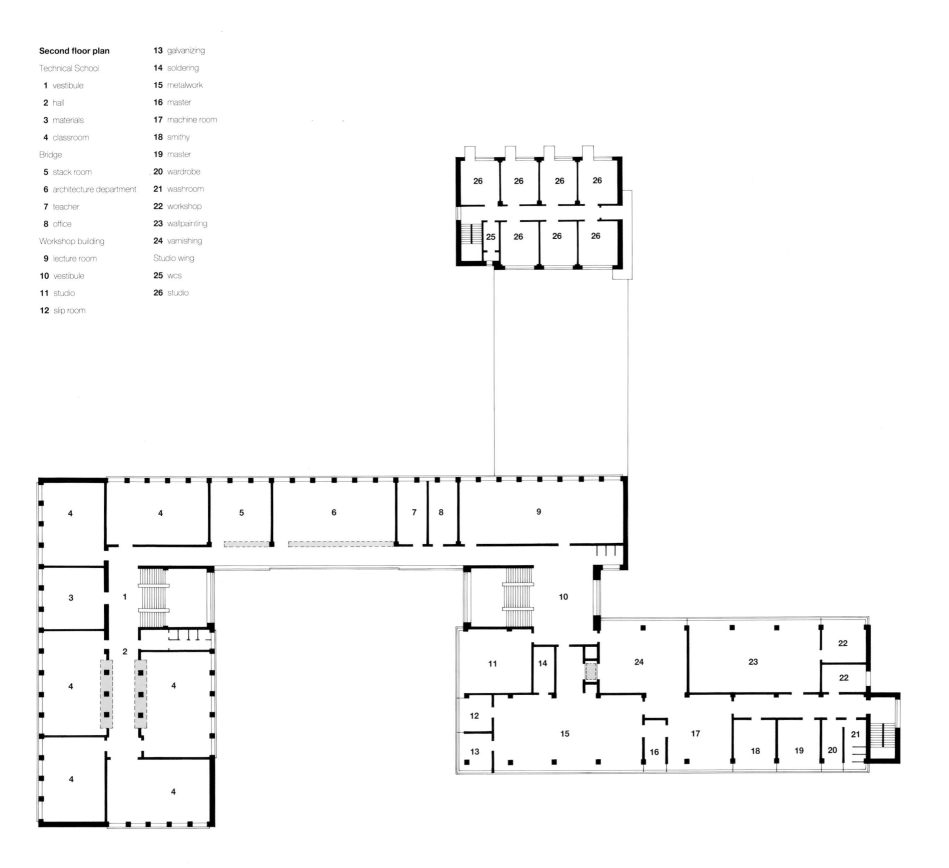

Second floor plan

Technical School

  1 vestibule
  2 hall
  3 materials
  4 classroom

Bridge

  5 stack room
  6 architecture department
  7 teacher
  8 office

Workshop building

  9 lecture room
  10 vestibule
  11 studio
  12 slip room

  13 galvanizing
  14 soldering
  15 metalwork
  16 master
  17 machine room
  18 smithy
  19 master
  20 wardrobe
  21 washroom
  22 workshop
  23 wallpainting
  24 varnishing

Studio wing

  25 wcs
  26 studio

Section

through studios and
workshop block

Sectional elevation

through auditorium

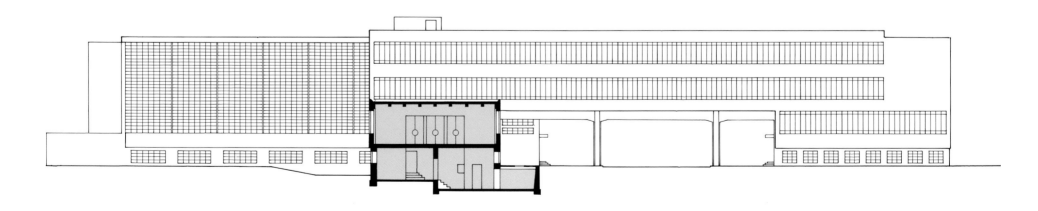

0   10 metres

0   30 feet

Axonometric projection

from the east

1 workshop block

2 auditorium and canteen

3 *Prellerhaus* studios

4 administration bridge

5 Technical College

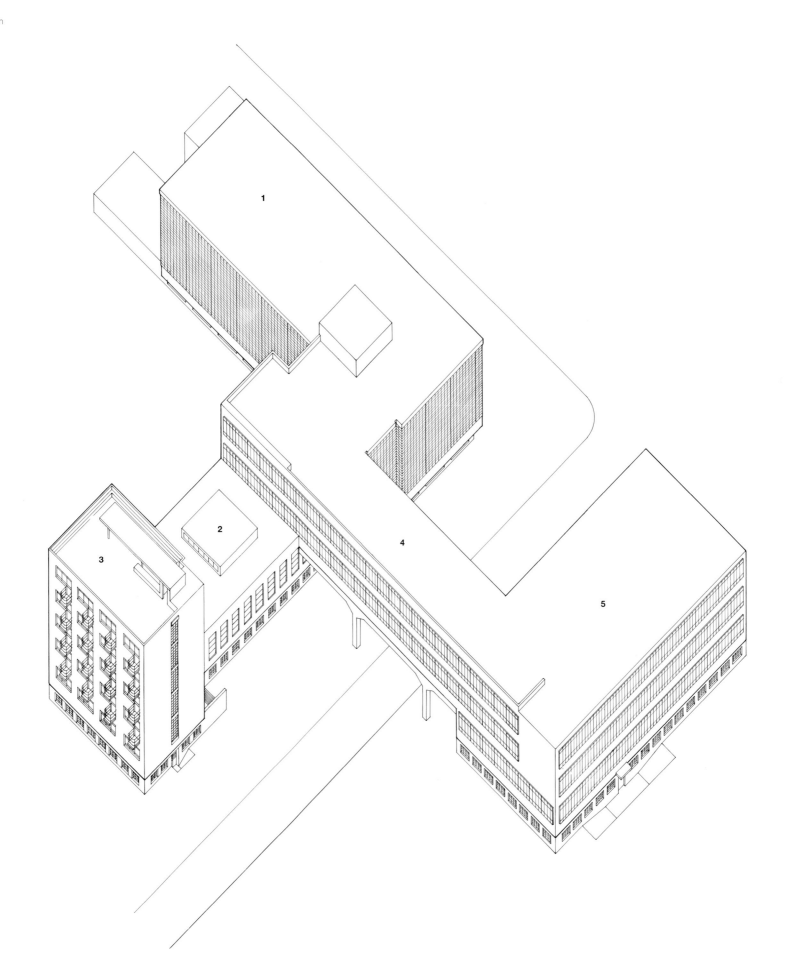

Elevation

Technical College

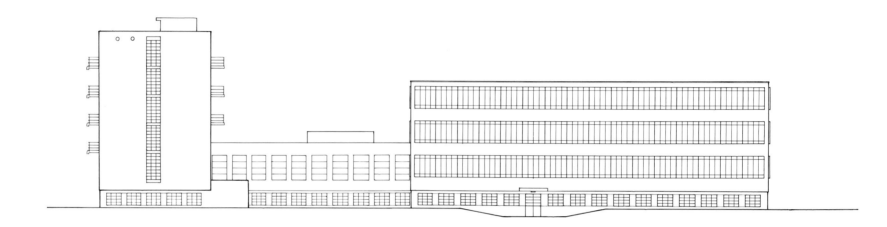

Elevation

main road of the Bauhaus

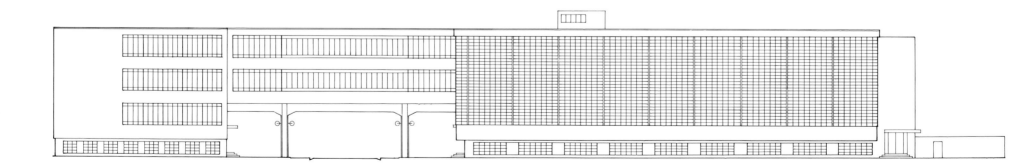

0   10 metres

0   30 feet

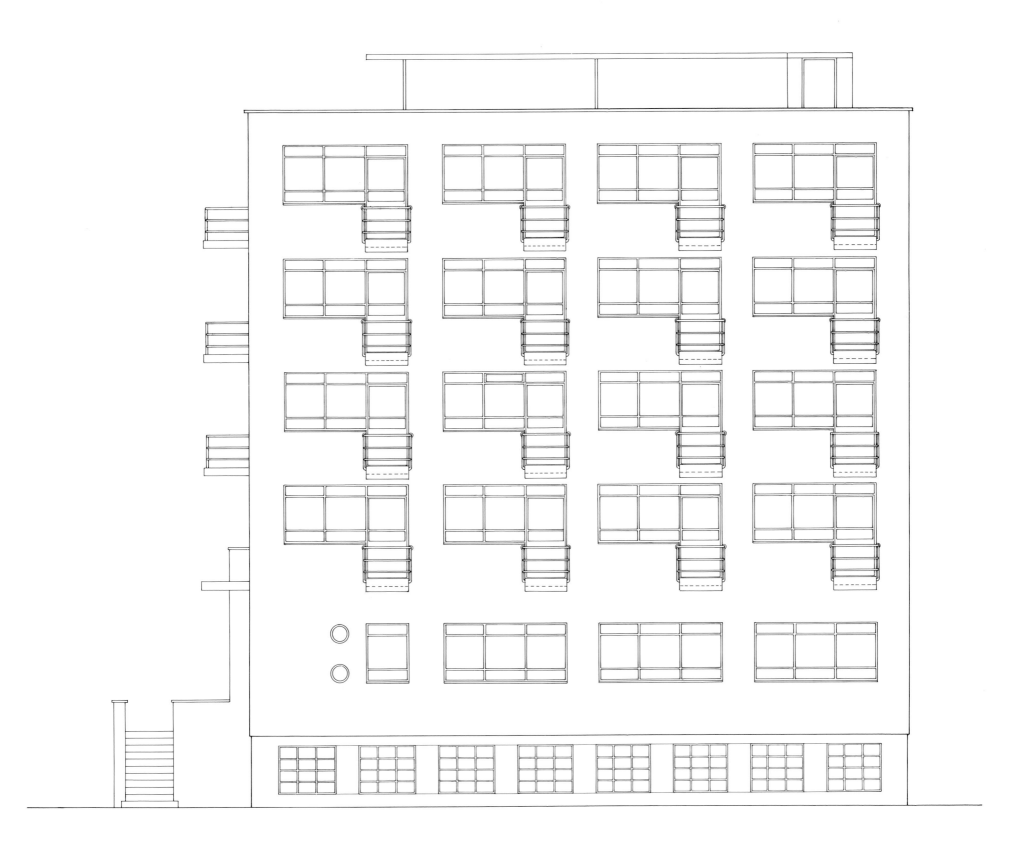

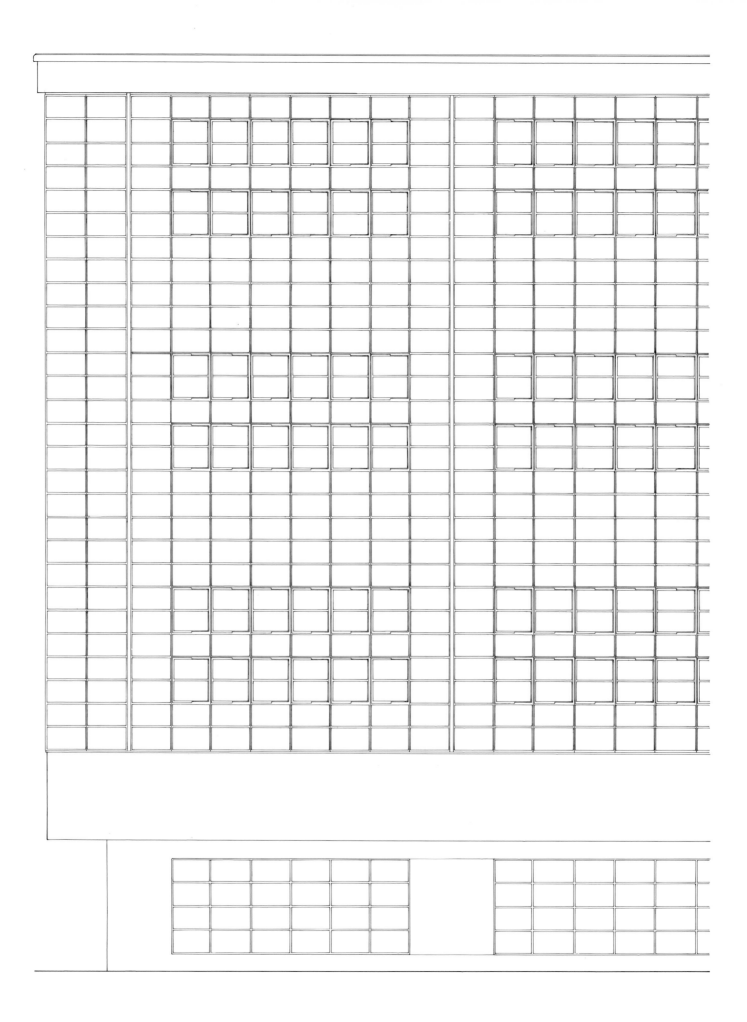

0   1 metre

0   3 feet

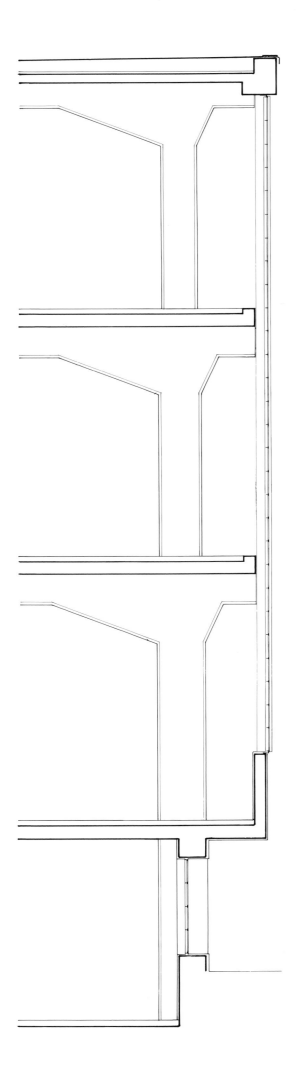

Probative section and details through perimeter of workshop block

Materials and construction as originally executed: reinforced concrete frame and floor slabs; brick infill walls; steel-framed windows, single-glazed; roofs covered with welded asphalt tiles on tortoleum-insulated base on roofs where walking was allowed, and with lacquered burlap on screed over tortoleum-insulated base where walking was not allowed.

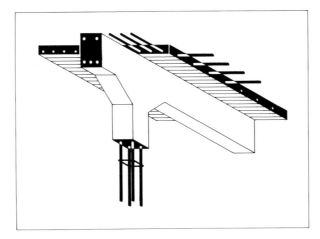

Structural detail

adapted from a contemporary source (1927)

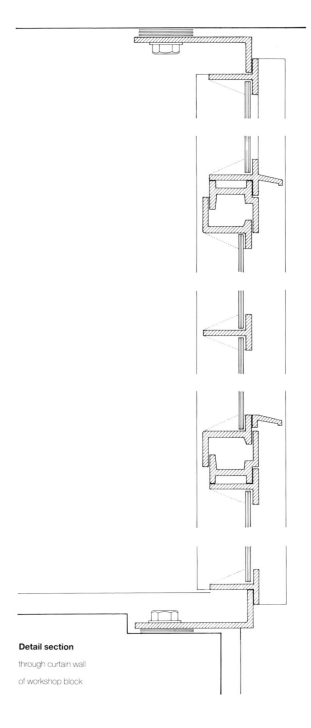

Detail section

through curtain wall of workshop block

Vertical section

through curtain wall of workshop block

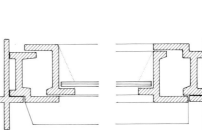

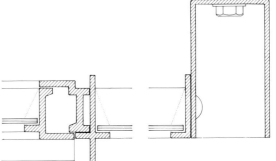

Typical plan

through curtain wall of workshop façade

Le Corbusier
Unité d'Habitation
Marseilles 1945–52

David Jenkins

Photography
Peter Cook; cover detail
supplied by VIEW, photograph
also by Peter Cook
Drawings
David Jenkins

The end of the war found Le Corbusier with little work; Soltan, like Hanning and André Wogenscky, who joined the atelier during this period, did so for little or no salary, while Le Corbusier courted new clients.

His first commissions came during 1945 from the Ministry of Reconstruction and Urbanism. Both were reconstruction studies; one for the town of La Rochelle-Pallice in north-west France, **2**; the other for St Dié in the Vosges. For St Dié, an industrial town which had been systematically razed by the retreating Nazis, Le Corbusier proposed a masterplan that followed the direction he had first defined in *La Ville Radieuse*, published in 1935, **3**, **4**. A linear pattern of eight free-standing Unités d'Habitation was imposed on either side of a civic and commercial centre incorporating shops, cafés, public buildings, administrative offices and a spirally-organized museum drawn directly from the Musée à Croissance Illimitée project of 1939. The eight Unités, each capable of housing 1600 inhabitants, were to provide working class apartments, designed according to the newly constituted ISAI programme (appartments sans affectation individuelle).[2]

After a painful period of consultation, however, Le Corbusier's masterplan was rejected, 'by the upper, middle and lower classes, the socialists and the communists';[3] but at St Dié he was to realize his first building in over ten years: a factory for the hat manufacturer Jacques Duval whose works had been destroyed in 1944. Apart from this 'one small pure flame'[4] Le Corbusier registered St Dié as a failure, although it had the benefit, as William Curtis has observed, of allowing him to play out in a real location the themes of monumentality and civic space, issues which had been underplayed in the 1933 CIAM Athens Charter and which would concern both Le Corbusier and CIAM in the next decade.[5]

It was against this troublesome backdrop that Le Corbusier embarked on what was to become a heroic struggle with undoubtedly the most fortuitous commission from this period, the Marseilles Unité d'Habitation, **5**. As Le Corbusier wrote later, 'If only the Marseilles block had been completed first, things would have turned out differently, and the reconstruction of Saint Dié ... would have been a dazzling demonstration of what the machine age could achieve'.[6]

1 Le Corbusier, photographed in 1953 when he was 65.
2 An aerial perspective study by Le Corbusier of La Rochelle-Pallice, north-west France, from the *Oeuvre Complète, 1938–46*. The scheme proposed a series of ten Unités d'Habitation and linear housing blocks in a new residential quarter to the west of the old centre of La Rochelle.

With the liberation of Paris, Le Corbusier reopened his atelier at 35 rue de Sèvres. Jerzy Soltan, a young Polish architect arriving for his first day of work there on 1 August 1945, recalls entering the cloister of the old Jesuit monastery to which the atelier was attached and climbing the gloomy staircase that led up to Le Corbusier's long, corridor-like, drafting room:

'On this summer day, the atelier was not only full of sun, the sound of birds and the rustling of leaves, it was also full of bric-à-brac ... broken and half-broken architectural models in various scales, rolls of drawings, drafting instruments and, of course, covering everything was a thick layer of dust. Dust had been gathering here for six years since the beginning of the war and the decay of the atelier into a débarras. It was awakening at this time to its new, post-war, life. The forward part of the atelier was more orderly. Along the outer wall and perpendicular to it were a few drafting tables, some stools and chairs. Drawings were pinned up on the "church wall"; facing the windows between the tables and the wall, a large iron stove, installed ad hoc, dominated the space. And in front of the stove, wearing indescribably dirty, formerly white, drafting overalls, reigned Gerald Hanning, Corbu's only collaborator at that time'.[1]

The Marseilles commission came, late in 1945, from Raoul Dautry, France's first post-war Minister for Reconstruction and Urbanism. Dautry was a long-standing friend, an enlightened patron and a convinced modernist. He had been largely responsible for the effective modernization of the French railway system in the 1930s and was exactly the kind of technocrat whom, before the war, Le Corbusier had envisaged as being amongst the standard bearers of the new machine age.

Their professional relationship had begun in 1939 when Dautry, as Minister for Armaments, commissioned Le Corbusier to build a Usine-Verte near Aubusson.[7] However, the entry of the Nazis into Paris on June 14 1940 stopped this project in its tracks and caused Le Corbusier, who happened to be in Aubusson at the time of the invasion, to retreat with his wife Yvonne and cousin Pierre Jeanneret to the village of Ozon in the Pyrénées.

This moment is symbolic also because it presaged the end of Le Corbusier's long-standing partnership with his cousin. Pierre Jeanneret left for Grenoble to join the Resistance[8] while Le Corbusier, following

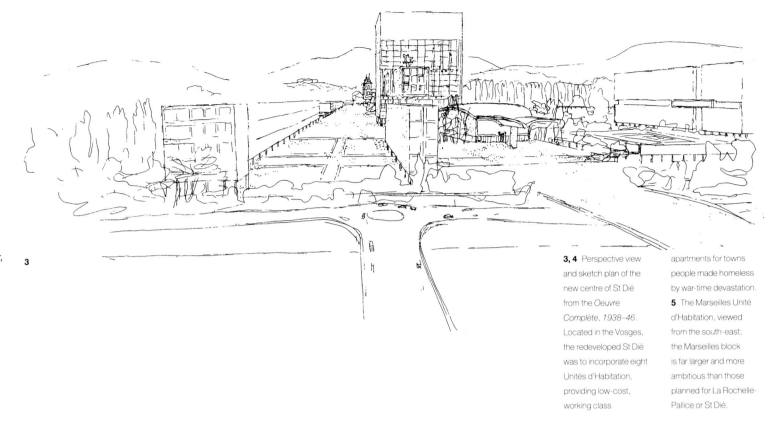

3

3, 4 Perspective view and sketch plan of the new centre of St Dié from the *Oeuvre Complète, 1938–46.* Located in the Vosges, the redeveloped St Dié was to incorporate eight Unités d'Habitation, providing low-cost, working class apartments for towns people made homeless by war-time devastation. **5** The Marseilles Unité d'Habitation, viewed from the south-east; the Marseilles block is far larger and more ambitious than those planned for La Rochelle-Pallice or St Dié.

5

the armistice and the advent of Free France, reacquainted himself with his former associates in the Syndicalist movement[9] and the Redressement Français, many of whom now occupied positions of power in the Vichy regime of Marshal Pétain.

Preparing for reconstruction

Le Corbusier's activities during the years of occupation can be seen as profoundly influential on the direction and shape that his post-war work in general, and the Unité project in particular, was to take. In 1953, he introduced his book on the project by proclaiming: 'During the occupation I didn't do as much as one square inch of planning. With all the devastation – houses, farms, indeed whole towns – there was plenty to be done. But I was not asked. Not a house, not a church, not a town hall or a museum. Nothing. I was in bad odour'.[10]

Though characteristically rhetorical, this claim does not quite ring true. In the spring of 1941, Le Corbusier was rewarded for his overtures to the Vichy government and found himself appointed to head a committee charged with preparing a plan for revitalizing the French housing industry. Alongside him was his old friend François de Pierrefeu with whom he collaborated to publish *La Maison des Hommes*, one of an astonishing number of books containing recommendations for the

reconstruction of France which Le Corbusier published in the period 1941–1944.

Le Corbusier assumed his role on the committee, in the face of obstruction from the entrenched conservative planners and architects, who predominated in the Vichy establishment. He persevered for several months, only to be summarily dismissed in July 1941. Frustrated by this experience, and unable to secure firm commissions, he turned instead to formulating his own theoretical basis for the coming French reconstruction programme.

La Maison des Hommes, together with a revised edition of the Athens Charter, which Le Corbusier hoped would sound a clarion call for French modernists, were his parting shots before he abandoned Vichy for Paris in July 1942. It was here, during the latter part of that year, that he set about assembling his own research group which became known as ASCORAL – Assemblée de Constructeurs pour une Rénovation Architecturale. ASCORAL attracted supporters of CIAM, many of whom were students of architecture, such as the Frenchman Roger Aujame who later joined the atelier at rue de Sèvres as one of the project team working on the Marseilles Unité.

From its first meeting in March 1943, ASCORAL spread its sphere of interest to comprise eleven groups, and further sub-

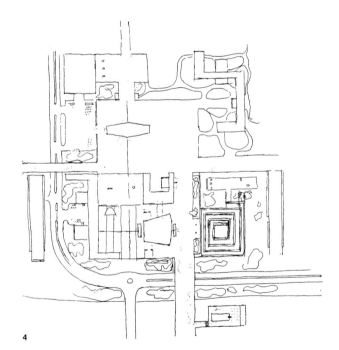

4

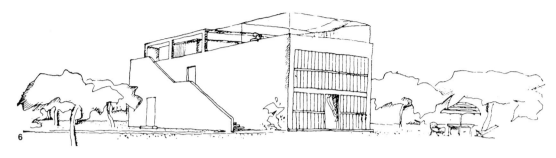

6

6, 7 Le Corbusier's generative Maison Citrohan as published in the *Oeuvre Complète, 1910–29* and as built at the Stuttgart Weissenhof Seidlung in 1927.

When Raoul Dautry became Minister for Reconstruction and Urbanism on 16 November 1944, Le Corbusier sent him a copy of this prospectus. He had hoped for a large prize from Dautry's portfolio; but the offer of building in the Communist-run city of Marseilles was a political move on Dautry's part, calculated to steer the overly ambitious Le Corbusier away from the great post-war urbanization programmes, such as that of the Seine valley which stretched from Paris to Le Havre (Le Havre, itself one of the largest reconstruction centres, had been awarded by Dautry to August Perret).

Years of development

The Unité d'Habitation can be seen as Le Corbusier's most significant contribution to social housing typology in so far as it offered a universal solution to the post-war European housing crisis; but its conception had already been followed by a long period of gestation by the time Le Corbusier received the Marseilles commission. It draws as much upon his experimental work with housing prototypes during the 1920s as upon his investigations into collective housing forms under ASCORAL. Indeed, Le Corbusier

claimed: 'This is the building I have wanted to build for twenty-five years'.[13]

In fact, some of the basic characteristics of the Marseilles apartments can be traced to his earliest work. The double-height living space, for example, a leitmotiv of Le Corbusier's domestic architecture, is to be found in his very first house, the Villa Fallet, in his native La Chaux-de-Fonds, completed in 1906 when he was eighteen years old. Here he groups the ground-floor living areas and first-floor living rooms around an open, double-height hall, a feature which had great currency in Arts and Crafts domestic architecture of the period.

The Maison Citrohan, **6, 7**, Le Corbusier's idealized maison-type first exhibited at the Salon d'Automne in 1922, famously expanded this generating idea by assimilating the typological characteristics of the Parisian artist's studio; typically, a long, split-level workshop space lit from one end by a large picture window. Le Corbusier also recalled another potent model for this arrangement, the bistro 'Legendre', located opposite the painter Ozenfant's studio on the rue Godot-de-Mauroy, where he and Ozenfant regularly used to dine.[14]

groups, with a wide range of concerns from the aesthetic education of children, vernacular art and folklore, to equipping the modern home, land use and urban planning. Le Corbusier chaired all its meetings.

Early in the war, Le Corbusier had advocated the mass-construction of simple self-build dwellings, 'Maisons Murondins',[11] which were designed to accommodate the influx of refugees from Belgium and Holland. This was a theme he returned to with ASCORAL in 1944. The Unité d'Habitation Transitoire[12] was one of a series of studies, intended this time to address the housing emergency faced by the displaced populations of towns and cities destroyed during the war, that can be seen as the natural successors to the Murondins project and as tentative steps on the way to Marseilles.

The publication of *Les Trois Etablissements Humains*, in 1944, summarized ASCORAL's shifting analysis. Le Corbusier began to plan in pan-European terms relying, as at St Dié, on patterns of development that had been propounded in the Athens Charter and *La Ville Radieuse*. The report envisaged a linear series of 'Radiant Cities', to be located between the major centres of population from Paris to Moscow, each with cultural, commercial and administrative centres, connected by secondary ribbons of industry and punctuated by tertiary radiant agricultural collectives.

7

The notion of the house as an open-ended mechanism, with a glazed front and closed sides, which underscores the entire development of the Unité principle, can also be traced in embryo to projects from Le Corbusier's Purist canon, for example, the Villa Meyer in Paris, 1925, the Villa Cook in Boulogne-sur-Seine, 1926 and the Maison Guitte in Antwerp, 1926.

However, it is to the Pavillon de l'Esprit Nouveau,[15] constructed at the 1925 Paris Exposition des Arts Décoratifs, that one must look for the first concrete realization of a model dwelling capable of being agglomerated to form apartment blocks of Immeubles Villas, **8**, **9**. Launched in stark opposition to the Art Deco interior which prevailed at the Exposition, the Pavillon can be seen as a concise summary of Le Corbusier's thesis to date. It was equipped with mass-produced, factory-made *objets-type*; furniture including the now iconic Thonet bentwood chair and was hung with paintings by Le Corbusier and Ozenfant. The whole composition was intended to convey a message of mechanical purity and economy. Le Corbusier's description of the Pavillon and the Immeubles Villas exhibit which

8

10

9

accompanied it, is revealing: 'The programme ... was as follows: the rejection of decorative art as such, accompanied by an affirmation that the sphere of architecture embraces every detail of household furnishing, the street as well as the house, and a wider world still beyond both. My intention was to illustrate how, by virtue of the selective principle (standardization applied to mass production), industry creates pure forms; and to stress the intrinsic value of this pure form of art that results from it. Secondly, to show the radical transformations and structural freedom that reinforced concrete and steel allow us to envisage in urban housing – in other words, to show that a dwelling can be standardized to meet the needs of men whose lives are standardized'.[16]

Le Corbusier frequently followed this pseudo-Darwinian line in his contributions to *l'Esprit Nouveau*, the magazine of the Purist movement that he co-edited with Ozenfant. The doctrine of 'Purism' and Le Corbusier's argument for a process of 'natural' mechanical selection is bound up with a neo-Platonic notion of the 'essence' of machine-made artefacts – bottles, glasses, pipes, musical instruments, etc. – whose role and form had become normative through evolutionary refinement. One of these *objets-type* finds later resonances in Le Corbusier's description of the Unité principle: the bottle,

as container rather than object, becoming a metaphor for the mass-produced dwelling.

Hand in hand with Le Corbusier's notion of perfected *objets-type* went a deterministic conception of an idealized 'homme-type' – 'l'homme poli vivant en ce temps-ci', who would be prepared for life in the new blocks: to 'savoir vivre' Le Corbusier added 'savoir habiter', a know how of dwelling which these inhabitants would acquire through education by those already versed in the new 'science' of housing.

Perhaps mindful of the disastrous results of introducing an inappropriate, largely rural working-class population into his ill-fated development at Pessac in 1925[17] which had been intended for middle-income families, **10**, he was to demand later, in the context of Marseilles, 'Get ready a social group which is fit to live in the Unité d'Habitation'.[18]

The Corbusian notion of the house as a 'machine à habiter', implicit in his description above, is equally open to misinterpretation. It has been viewed by his critics as indicative of a Fordian desire to reduce both dweller and dwelling to the level of production-line mechanisms, an interpretation which Le Corbusier invited initially by the use of the punning name Citrohan – literally, a house like a car. A more precise vehicle for this analogy might have been one of Ettore Bugatti's hand-crafted, silent running saloons, which, though

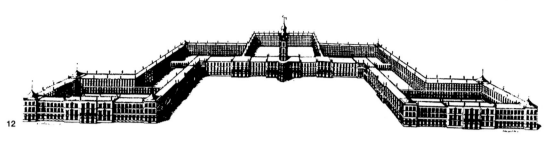

12

11 Transformations of the ocean liner and the palace, published in *Précisions* in 1929; the ocean liner is a recurrent Corbusian metaphor.
12 The phalanstère as proposed by Victor Considerant in c.1834; Le Corbusier was well acquainted with this and other 19th century public housing models.
13 The Immeuble Clarté, Geneva, 1930–32, has a steel frame of entirely standardized components.
14 The Pavillon Suisse, at the Cité Universitaire, Paris, 1930–32.

Soviet avant-garde) the abolition of the single-family dwelling. Rather, he intended that it should be remade, and located within a collective mechanism that would allow it to be systematized and sustained.

The Immeubles Villas prototype, which formed an integral part of Le Corbusier's La Ville Contemporaine studies,[21] grew directly out of the Citrohan project. From the early 1920s Le Corbusier and Pierre Jeanneret had begun to investigate ways of collectivizing ideal dwelling types into high-rise, well-serviced apartment blocks. Such blocks were to be provided with communal facilities in the manner of a grand hotel or, better, a great ocean-going liner, **11**, a metaphor for which Le Corbusier had enduring affection: the suggestion of the 'good life' and ship-board benefits of light, air and health-inducing activity are adopted here as central themes.[22]

Each Immeuble apartment is provided with its own terrace and hanging garden, and each family has free access to a wide range of amenities including restaurants, shops, children's nurseries, club rooms and sports facilities, all of which were to be incorporated eventually at Marseilles. Having banished the family maid, Le Corbusier envisaged instead a crew of domestic servants who would serve each 'cell' like cabin stewards on-board ship.

From the early 1930s, however, following the CIAM conference in Brussels, with its emphasis on a new objectivity, a 'Neue Sachlichkeit', Le Corbusier began to shift his investigations away from the provision of housing for an affluent urban middle class, towards the more egalitarian and far-reaching concept of the Ville Radieuse. The apartment buildings of this radiant city are more austere than their earlier counterparts; Le Corbusier focuses on standardization, economy and numbers of units as his new priorities.

Arranged in continuous blocks à redents – with setbacks – they can be seen to reflect the influence of German and Soviet social housing schemes of the period. However, as von Moos has shown[23] this monumental conception has deeper roots which go down as far as the post-revolutionary concept of the phalanstère, a 'Versailles for the people', as propounded by Charles Fourier in the early nineteenth century. And the rues à redents as laid out by Le Corbusier in *La Ville Radieuse* look remarkably like Victor Considerant's well-publicized proposal for a phalanstère of c.1834, **12**. Le Corbusier refers himself

13

potential models for serial production, more significantly propagated an image appropriate to the times.

However, as Stanislaus von Moos has observed, in French philosophy, the machine has been synonymous with the notion of a rational ideal since the eighteenth century, and Le Corbusier adopted it as a cosmological and philosophical metaphor of great dignity.[19]

Such a complex sense of physical and spiritual order is compatible with Le Corbusier's reliance on monastic models for the activities which he isolated to characterize the dualism of daily life: those that are private and located within the dwelling, and those which are performed collectively within the community. Although it is perhaps more accurate to turn this analysis on its head and to say that it was Le Corbusier's fascination with the contemplative aspects of monastic life (which he first observed at the age of nineteen on a visit to the monastery at Ema near Florence, in 1907), that led him to his basic set of definitions, most importantly that of the dwelling unit or 'cell'.[20]

Notwithstanding his fascination with the discipline imposed by monasticism, and his belief that the traditional bourgeois household, with its servants and domestic clutter, was obsolescent, Le Corbusier never proposed (as did his contemporaries in the

14

11

to Fourier and his 'wild ideas' of houses supplied with main services in his book on the Marseilles Unité.[24]

At this point, Le Corbusier also introduced into mass-housing the 'free plan' and the flexible use of living space which are implicit in the Maison Domino project and had been explored in the Citrohan 2 houses completed at the Stuttgart Weissenhof Seidlung in 1927. The à redents blocks incorporated sliding partitions capable of converting the living area into separate rooms according to family need and provided built-in furniture and equipment to maximize the limited space available in the cabin-like rooms.

It is the liner-like quality of Le Corbusier's first fragmentary hybrid of the Ville Contemporaine and Ville Radieuse studies – the Immeuble Clarté in Geneva, **13**, 1930–32 – that first impresses.[25] Commissioned by the Geneva metals manufacturer Edmond Wanner, who also acted as the building contractor, the Immeuble Clarté has a steel frame of entirely standardized components, Le Corbusier's preferred, but abandoned, method for constructing the Marseilles Unité. It can be seen as his first convincing case for constructional systemization, though as

15

15 The Cité de Refuge, Paris, 1932–33, a building that exemplifies the rhetoric of Le Corbusier's standardization ideal. **16** A block with brise-soleil figured façades from Le Corbusier's set of Algiers Obus projects from the period 1930–38, published in the *Oeuvre Complète*, 1938–46.

William Curtis has observed, it is less evocative of that ideal than its far less standardized contemporaries, the Pavillon Suisse and the Cité de Refuge, **14**, **15**.[26]

The fact that the drawings relating to many of these early schemes have been archived amongst the Unité drawings is indicative of Le Corbusier's reliance on them during the developmental stages of the Unité's design. What sets the Marseilles Unité apart from these projects, however, is the scale of its conception and the boldness of its execution.

Towards a synthesis

It was whilst developing a series of large-scale urbanization projects, including proposals for Nemours and Algiers, from the early 1930s onwards, that Le Corbusier began to employ the term 'une nouvelle Unité d'Habitation'.[27] His concern then, as in 1945, was to deliver a radical solution to the problem of collective housing in both architectural and urban terms.

The concept of the Unité d'Habitation as developed for Marseilles is rooted in another urban and architectural model, the vertical garden city. This was a proposition dating from *La Ville Radieuse* and codified by ASCORAL in *Propos d'Urbanisme* (first published in 1946), and reiterated by Le Corbusier in his book on the Marseilles Unité.[28] The vertical garden city represents

a synthesis of the two models of urban development which have dominated in Europe since the end of the nineteenth century: the suburban garden city and the city proper – 'la grande ville'.

From the 'horizontal' garden city Le Corbusier took the concept of the individual dwelling and the relationship between architecture and nature; from the city proper he distilled the notions of complexity and density and added to them the idea of the machine à habiter.

The basic arrangement of this new model was simple. Raised upon 'terrains artificiels' and supported on 'pilotis', individual housing units would be assembled within a highly serviced block. To give form to this arrangement, Le Corbusier followed two convergent paths. The first involved drawing together the conclusions of his earlier research projects ranging from the Immeubles Villas and the à redents blocks of La Ville Radieuse (from which the Marseilles Unité's alternating apartment section can be seen to derive)[29] to the Algiers Obus plan blocks, with their brise-soleil figured façades, **16**. The second path required him to edit his own architectural vocabulary to comprise: *pilotis*, *rue intérieure*, the split-level living unit, the loggia and the roof terrace. Via this adaptive process Le Corbusier was able to clarify a new, synthetic, urban object.

16

17 Le Corbusier's first proposal for a site in the Madrague quarter, published in the *Oeuvre Complète, 1938–46*. Overlooking the old port of Marseilles, it incorporated three discrete blocks, only one of which is indicative of the direction that the Unité project was to take.

18 The second project, published alongside the first proposal, was for a site on the Boulevard Michelet opposite the site selected finally. The complementary shops, nursery school, clubs and other amenities are arranged at ground level as discrete entities prior to their envelopment within the Unité block.

Le Corbusier's objective was for the project to be innovative in a number of specific areas: in an urban context, in the way that it challenged the traditional housing block; on a spatial and functional level; in its construction methods, which he geared to industrial processes controlled by the use of a new dimensional system derived from the Modulor; and in the use of new materials which would in turn allow the possibility of large-scale prefabrication.

The aims of the Unité d'Habitation, declared Le Corbusier, were two-fold, 'The first: to provide with peace and solitude before the sun, space and greenery, a dwelling which will be the perfect receptacle for the family. The second: to set up in God's good nature beneath the sky and in the sun, a magisterial work of architecture, the product of rigour, grandeur, nobility, happiness and elegance'.[30]

Le Corbusier was assisted by two bodies which worked together under his direction: ASCORAL and ATBAT (Atelier des Batisseurs) a technical organization which Le Corbusier founded in mid-1946 with André Wogenscky, Jacques LeFèvre, Marcel Py and the Russian-educated engineer Vladimir Bodiansky. The scale of the task faced by the thirty-strong ATBAT team can be measured against the astonishing number of drawings produced to describe the Unité: 2785 separate (and often contradictory) sheets for this building alone. ATBAT comprised a works management section initially under Py, but later under Wogenscky, an architectural section under Wogenscky, an administrative and supervisory group, originally under LeFèvre but, again, taken over later by Wogenscky, and a technical team directed by Bodiansky.[31]

Bodiansky had settled in France after fleeing Moscow for Paris during the October Revolution, and had met Le Corbusier during the war; his complex and varied background made him a natural candidate to fill the void left by the departure of Pierre Jeanneret. He had been an aircraft designer, a railway engineer and chief engineer for the 'Mopin' building prefabrication system; he had also co-directed the construction of the Quarry Hill estate in Leeds, 1937, and become acquainted with all aspects of architecture. He was the archetypal architect-engineer.[32]

Idealism amid chaos

Between August 1945, the date of the commission, and September 1947, the date when building began, four different sites were proposed to Le Corbusier by as many Ministers of Reconstruction. During the immediate post-war period France suffered great political and economic instability, with governments forming and falling almost routinely: ten successive governments came and went during the course of the project from 1945 to 1951.

Raoul Dautry had resigned in January 1946, to be replaced in quick succession by M. F. Billoux and M. C. Tillon, a Communist, who was responsible for ratifying the commission in March 1947 following approval of the contract drawings. He in turn resigned in May 1947, four months before construction work commenced.

The first site suggested to Le Corbusier was located in the Madrague quarter, a working class, industrial zone overlooking the old port of Marseilles.[33] It allowed him to resume in earnest the studies of structural systems and apartment types that he had begun with ASCORAL. He proposed initially a series of three distinct blocks, **17**. The first, and smallest, comprised thirty-two apartments based on the Immeubles Villas model; the second was a high-rise gallery access slab reminiscent of the Pavillon Suisse, 1930–32, and the third was the Unité in embryo.[34]

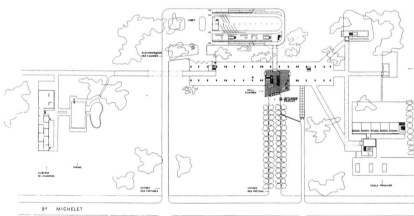

The preliminary project for the second site, located in the comfortably middle-class 8th arrondissement of Marseilles, was drawn in its entirety during 1946. This scheme redefined the proposal from three blocks to a single 'Unité d'Habitation de grandeur conforme' – a Unité of the appropriate size. This block was placed parallel with Boulevard Michelet, which forms the great north–south axis through Marseilles, and was complemented at ground level by a school, clubs, shops, a swimming pool and other amenities, **18**.[35] A third site, located in the Saint Barnabe area to the east of the city was considered briefly but not studied in great detail.

The fourth, and actual, site is located to the west of Boulevard Michelet which in the 1940s was still a rough terrain populated by olive trees and cypresses. Le Corbusier's response to this location took up the general form of the preliminary project, intended originally for the second site on the other side of the boulevard. He made three major modifications, however: the plans were revised to satisfy the new conditions of site access and orientation; and many of the amenities which had previously been located at the foot of the building were integrated

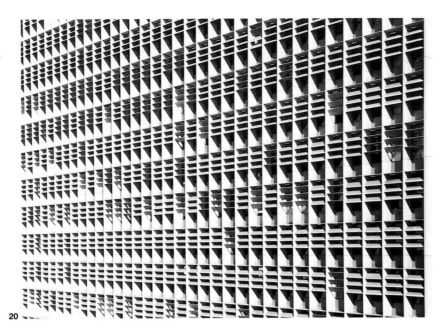

20

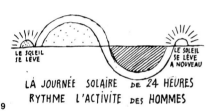

19

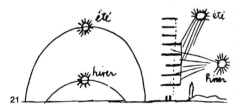

21

within the main structure of the block itself. It was in this final position that Le Corbusier refined the constituent elements of the Unité principle as built: the mass-produced apartment, an independent supporting skeleton and brise-soleil sun screening.

The brise-soleil

The brise-soleil represents a new departure in Le Corbusier's work, a move away from the pre-war quest for openness as represented by the fênetre-en-longeur, or the transparency of the all-glass façade as realized in the Immeuble Clarté. In *La Maison des Hommes* Le Corbusier began to explore a spiritual reciprocity between light and dark, day and night, **19**, and to define the equilibrium between patterns of human activity and leisure that follow from it. He weaves a sustaining myth around this 'harmonious solar day' in *Le Poème de l'Angle Droit*, a prose poem in which he draws out spiritual themes and obsessions concerned with the interplay of natural forces: earth and water, sun and moon, shadow and light.

The brises-soleil also bring with them a new muscularity which characterizes Le Corbusier's post-war work. They are the heavy, passive and low-technology counterpart of the mechanical environmental control systems implicit in the notion of the machine à habiter. They can also be seen as

overtly defensive devices, constituting a rough armoured zone that wraps the more structured and rational realm within and conveys an overwhelming sense of compositional unity and strength.

From the early 1930s, Le Corbusier had experimented with external sun screening devices with two projects for fierce sunny climates, a housing development in Barcelona and the first of many blocks in Algiers. It was the extreme environmental challenge of Rio de Janiero, however, that produced the first concrete example. The Ministry of Education and Health, **20**, designed in association with Oscar Niemeyer, features brises-soleil on its northern, sun-facing elevation in a system comprising fixed vertical fins and adjustable horizontal louvres.[36]

At Marseilles, the brises-soleil are fixed with the aim of screening direct sunlight from the apartment glazing in the summer months, while admitting the lower winter sun. Le Corbusier justified this system in sketches, **21**, **22**, and elaborate sun path diagrams, concluding, in line with the 1951 CIAM Athens Charter, that every apartment should benefit from at least two hours of sunlight on the shortest day of the year.

He placed the Unité at an oblique angle in relation to Boulevard Michelet so as to shelter the apartments from the force of the Mistral, which sweeps down into Marseilles from the

19 The harmonious solar day; a sketch which was published by Le Corbusier in *La Maison des Hommes*.
20 Brises-soleil as incorporated in the Ministry of Education and Health, Rio de Janiero, 1936, designed in collaboration with Oscar Niemeyer.
21, 22 Brises-soleil as justified in sketch form by Le Corbusier in *La Maison des Hommes* and impressed in the concrete at Marseilles. The upper and lower arcs indicate the path of the summer and winter sun respectively.

22

with the provision of what he termed the 'essential joys' of sun, space and verdure; and one might add 'view'. As ever, preserving the 'ideal' was more important to him than accommodating the real.

Ultimately, since the brises-soleil on the east and west façades are of equal depth and position, despite their diametrically-opposed orientation, one is forced to conclude that they have more to do with art than science. They are applied to great sculptural effect in a brilliantly polychromatic modulating pattern; the crate-like concrete forms articulating a protective loggia before each apartment, **23**.

The Modulor

It has been claimed of the Marseilles Unité[38] that its colour scheme was adopted to disguise errors in the window proportions and thus to reassert the regulating order of the Modulor, although this is an observation that seems more apposite in the case of the dazzle-painted Berlin Unité where it is known that Le Corbusier was forced by the city authorities to compromise the design. In Marseilles, the Modulor generates the building's fifteen controlling dimensions giving the block an immense formal clarity.

Le Corbusier had first employed the Modulor in the design of the Duval Factory at St Dié, and intended that it should become a proportional regulator not simply in his own work, but universally throughout architecture. He also advocated its use in industry as a system for standardizing product sizes: sheet paper, for example.

Published in two versions in 1948 and 1955 respectively, the Modulor, like the Unité itself, can be seen as the result of an idea long in gestation. From the early 1920s, in *l'Esprit Nouveau* and *Vers une Architecture*, Le Corbusier had established the importance of geometric 'regulating lines' as one of the essential keys to composition. As William Curtis has shown,[39] while Le Corbusier was following in the footsteps of Werkbund theorists who, before World War One, had advocated modular systems of measurement as a means to 'civilize' the new reality of mass-production, the Modulor was more than simply a design tool; it is a philosophical emblem of Le Corbusier's commitment to discovering an underlying order in architecture equivalent to that found in nature.

The Modulor is essentially an anthropometric system, resulting from a

23 The Unité's brises-soleil are applied in crate-like concrete forms which articulate protective loggias in front of each apartment.
24, 25 Modular man as impressed in the Marseilles concrete and as sketched by Le Corbusier in the *Oeuvre Complète, 1946–52*. The Modulor generates the Unité's fifteen controlling dimensions in the vertical and horizontal planes, giving the block great formal clarity.

north. Although logical in that respect, this positioning tends to undermine the argument for the brises-soleil, which Le Corbusier applied equally to the east, west and south façades. It has been argued that the Marseilles Unité would have gained greater benefit from its brises-soleil if the block had been rotated through 90 degrees so that the long elevation faced south or south-east, allowing low morning sunlight to penetrate the plan while excluding the hot midday sun.[37] In this way, only the short apartment elevation would face the intense evening sun.

As built, however, the brises-soleil on the west-facing elevation allow two hours of solar penetration, from 3 to 5pm in the summer months and little more than 20 minutes of direct sunlight per day in the winter cycle. The apartments at the southern end of the block, by contrast, are completely shaded from April to September, but benefit from up to eight hours of sunlight in the winter months.

Naturally, the double-ended nature of the great majority of the Unité's apartments and the alternating arrangement of living rooms with bedrooms across the block makes its optimum placement in terms of sun screening alone very difficult. It is a common criticism of the Unité that those apartments whose living rooms face east are too dark, and those facing west are too bright. But Le Corbusier had to reconcile the question of orientation

classically Corbusian synthesis of ideas and influences as diverse as Vitruvian geometry and musical notation. Modulor man, as impressed in the concrete at Marseilles by Le Corbusier, **24, 25,** is the twentieth century inheritor of Vitruvian man as drawn by Leonardo da Vinci. Precisely six feet tall (the Modulor harmonized both metric and imperial measures) he stands with his arm raised inside a square whose major subdivisions are controlled by the golden section and whose smaller subdivisions are generated by the Fibonacci series. In later versions (the red and blue series) Le Corbusier introduced a pair of interspiralling dimensional scales which, in principle, would generate the proportions and dimensions of everything from door handle, to door, to room, to block, and eventually to the spaces between blocks themselves.

Le Corbusier often quoted in its favour Albert Einstein, who told him that the Modulor made 'the good likely and the bad unlikely'. But it is known from Wogenscky[40] that in practise Le Corbusier insisted that it should be used as a working instrument and not as a 'machine for manufacturing harmony': 'Having become accustomed to the Modulor in the rue de Sèvres workshop, we would

24

often respond when Le Corbusier criticized our drawings by saying "But it is done according to the Modulor", and then Le Corbusier would answer, "To hell with the Modulor. When it doesn't work you shouldn't use it"'. Ever the artist, he was not afraid to trust his eye when he felt that a dimension or proportion was wrong.

Béton brut
In construction, as with proportion, Le Corbusier was prepared to be pragmatic. Although his preference for the Marseilles Unité had been for steel-framed construction, he settled on reinforced concrete when steel proved unobtainable due to post-war shortages and a lack of funds. Reinforced concrete was by no means a new material in his architecture, however. The Maison Domino of 1915 had proposed a universal concrete-framed system capable of being clad and infilled in a variety of ways; and, since the 1920s, Le Corbusier and Pierre Jeanneret (who worked in August Perret's office from 1920–22) had become experts in concrete construction. Indeed, the five points of Le Corbusier's Purist syntax can be seen to stem from the development of the concrete frame principle.

It is likely also that Le Corbusier had already begun to change his mind. He had explored the use of reinforced concrete as an

expressive medium in the Pavillon Suisse and in the little Maison de Weekend of 1935. It was during this period that Le Corbusier began to accrue a collection of rough, natural *objets-trouvés* whose forms begin to find echoes in his work. The béton brut *pilotis* of the Pavillon Suisse, for example, have a sensuous bone-like cross section hinting at an anthropomorphism that finds full expression in the Marseilles Unité.

As Reyner Banham has observed, with the Marseilles Unité Le Corbusier abandoned the pre-war fiction that reinforced concrete was a precise machine-age material and recognized it for what it was: 'a messy soup of suspended dusts, grits and slumpy aggregate, mixed and poured under conditions subject to the weather and human fallibility'.[41]

In the 1920s, Le Corbusier had maintained the conceit of precision by rendering over the roughness and inaccuracies of the concrete with a seamless coating of plaster and paint. In Marseilles, however, in the midst of a shortage of materials and skills, and faced with a building industry which was just beginning to reform itself, Le Corbusier seized the reality of concrete and by an almost alchemical process of transformation, reinvented it as a rough and tectonically neutral plastic material.

In the hands of French masters of the technique such as Hennebique or Perret,

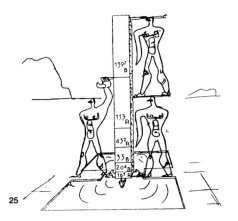

25

26 The *pilotis*, external staircase and hull of the Unité are all of cast concrete. Le Corbusier arranged the formwork and pre-cast elements in carefully predetermined patterns, which were calculated to impose a rough, rusticated order over the surface of the building.

27 Small rock-like outcrops on the roof deck mimic the massive mountain forms beyond and reinforce the notion of concrete as a natural material, analogous to stone.

stone and constituted literally from elements as old as the earth itself: the miniature rocky outcrops on the Unité's roof deck offer a witty illustration of this notion, echoing faintly as they do the massive mountain forms that lie behind the Marseilles skyline, **27**.

Others, notably John Farmer, have argued that Le Corbusier's overwhelming change of emphasis from the lightness of his Purist canon to the heaviness of the post-war work lies in the events and imagery of the Second World War. He notes compelling idiomatic similarities between the compositions of the Ronchamp Chapel, **28**, **29**, with its battered and perforated south wall, or the aggressive 'light cannons' and pill-box like parloirs in the defensive inner court of La Tourette, **30**, with the massive reinforced concrete structures that held strategic positions along the Maginot Line and peppered the European coast: 'As he had transformed images of the aero-engine and aeroplane into Utopian machine-age buildings of lightness and openness, so now Le Corbusier, after the terrible war, and in the lull of a peace that did not feel secure, must have seized on the image of the bunker and the air-raid shelter, as being psychologically as well as physically secure enough shelter for "an embattled human presence in the world"'.[43]

In this last phrase, Farmer echoes Vincent Scully, who finds resonances with Le Corbusier's expressive programme in the Classical roots of Humanist myth:

'Although the individual apartment units are expressed, ... all user scale elements, such as doors and windows, which normally make us read buildings not as sculptural creatures but as hollow containers of human activity, are suppressed, so that the building, like a Greek temple with its peripheral colonnade has only sculptural scale. It thus stands upon its muscular legs as an image of human uprightness and dignifies all its individual units within a single embodiment of the monumental human force which makes them possible. The high space of each apartment looks out towards the mountains or the sea, and it is in relation to the mountains and the sea that the building as a whole should be seen. This is the larger Hellenic environment it creates. So perceived it is a Humanist building, as we emphatically associate ourselves with it, in the contrasting landscape as a standing body analogous to our own'.[44]

26

concrete had long been used to great structural effect and economy of means, although skilled labour was habitually lavished on the preparation of complex and costly formwork to ensure a high degree of accuracy and refinement. In post-war southern France, however, Le Corbusier was denied such luxuries. He explored instead the strengths and limitations of the material, allowing the rough wooden boards that were available for shuttering to leave fossil-like impressions of knots and grain in the concrete surface. He arranged the forms themselves in carefully predetermined patterns, calculated to impart a rough rusticated order over the expanse of the building, **26**. Le Corbusier's 'béton brut' has in Banham's phrase 'a rugged grandeur' resonant with the scale and surface of the Homeric ruins of the Meditteranean coast.

Banham attempted further to identify the historical memories excited by Le Corbusier's béton brut: 'The coarseness of the surface, the pattern of plankwork and the scale of the building produced an architectural texture that was not only interesting in itself, but, under the hard glare of the Meditteranean sun gave something of the effect of the coarse travertine and giant scale of the apses of Michelangelo's St Peter's in Rome'.[42]

Indeed, Le Corbusier saw concrete as a profoundly natural material, analogous to

27

28

29

30

28, 29 The Chapel of Notre-Dame-du-Haut, Ronchamp, 1950–55, with its battered south wall and aggressive tank-trap-like concrete forms is redolent of the war-time fortifications that peppered northern France.

30 The Dominican Monastery of Sainte-Marie-de-la-Tourette, Eveux, 1957–60; 'light-cannon' rooflights above the Sacristy.

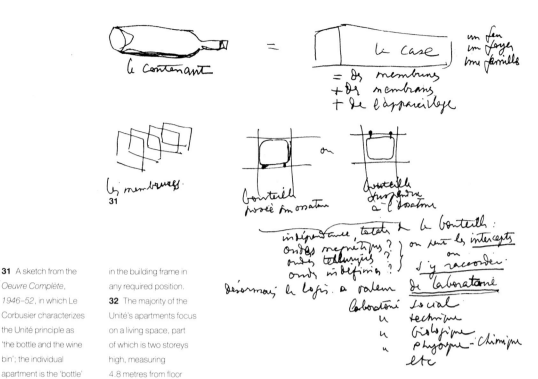

31 A sketch from the *Oeuvre Complète, 1946–52*, in which Le Corbusier characterizes the Unité principle as 'the bottle and the wine bin'; the individual apartment is the 'bottle' capable of being stowed in the building frame in any required position. **32** The majority of the Unité's apartments focus on a living space, part of which is two storeys high, measuring 4.8 metres from floor to ceiling.

The bottle and the wine-bin

Providentially, it was during the sketch stages of development that Le Corbusier was forced to abandon the steel-framed solutions he had been investigating and to opt instead for concrete. The first apartment studies published in the *Oeuvre Complète*[45] evoke the possibility of a free-plan arrangement and structural frame similar to that of the Immeuble Clarté. The contrary concept of a modular, lattice-like structure, capable of being infilled with a range of prefabricated cells, was introduced at this point by Jean Prouvé and enthusiastically pursued by Le Corbusier and Bodiansky. It was Prouvé, also, who first proposed that the individual cells should be factory produced.[46]

Le Corbusier's own characterization of this principle rests most memorably on an *objet-type* metaphor borrowed from his Purist vocabulary: the bottle and the wine bin, **31**. Here he portrays it as a wine bottle which may be taken as a container in the way that the dwelling unit is a container: 'A bottle may contain champagne, beaune or just vin ordinaire, but the one we are talking about invariably contains a family … It must be designed with the same rigorous observance of order as if it were a machine, an aeroplane, a motor car, or any other product of modern civilization… And having made our bottle, the dwelling, we can plump it down under an apple tree in Normandy or under a pine tree in the Jura. We can equally well push it into a pigeon-hole, that is to say into a space on the fifth or seventeenth floor of a framework … we can put it anywhere we like in what we might call the supporting skeleton. Or more simply a wine-bin. We just stow the bottle away in the bin'.[47]

In the Marseilles Unité, this 'wine-bin' principle allows a total of 337 apartments to be stowed in a framework eighteen storeys high. There are twenty-three variants on a basic apartment-type, ranging from those for single people and childless couples to those for families with up to eight children. Typically, the apartments are composed from three basic accommodational elements: a kitchen/living room, the parents' bedroom and bathroom and the childrens' bedrooms and showers. These elements are either manipulated, or added and subtracted to achieve the required range of dwelling sizes and types.

The majority of the apartments are dual aspect and oriented east–west, with the parents' and childrens' rooms occupying opposite ends of the plan, in the broad part of the 'bottle' and the neck respectively: if the parents' bedroom and living room face east, the childrens' rooms face west and vice versa. Those apartments located at the southern end of the building are single aspect and have the childrens' rooms placed alongside the parents' and living rooms rather than in line with them. There are no apartments at the northern, windward, end of the block.

Like the Citrohan and Esprit-Nouveau prototypes, the Unité apartments focus on a living room, part of which is two-storeys high, measuring 4.8 metres from floor to ceiling, **32**. In the most successful configuration, the lower part of this space, 2.26 metres high, serves as a dining area and kitchen; the living room and kitchen are integrated as far as possible, establishing the kitchen as the symbolic 'hearth' in the plan. A low, bar-like built-in unit mediates between the kitchen and dining areas, allowing those in the kitchen to maintain a conversation with family or friends at the dining table. This unit can be opened from either side to allow dishes from the kitchen to be stacked after washing-up, or retrieved from the dining side prior to laying the table.

The Unité kitchens were designed in close collaboration with Charlotte Perriand in what was her first project with Le Corbusier since 1937. Perriand, with some limited input from Prouvé, was responsible for the design of furniture, fixtures and fittings throughout the Unité's apartments although the kitchens are clearly the most important element in terms of both equipment and technical advancement, **33**.

Aside from Jean Prouvé, Perriand acknowledged the influence of American designers including Charles Eames whose work with light-weight laminated materials underscores much of the Unité's fitted furniture design.[48] The Unité's kitchens also set new standards outside of the USA in their provision of mechanical services and appliances; artificially-lit and ventilated, they are in Wogenscky's phrase, 'little labour-saving laboratories'[49] where everything is in easy reach. Each kitchen was originally equipped with an electric cooker, an ice chest (there was no refrigerator, but ice was delivered daily) and a double sink, part of which was plumbed directly into the building's waste-disposal system.

The apartments are narrow, 'like wagons-lit' as some critics would have it, set out on an internal module of 3.66 metres. But this

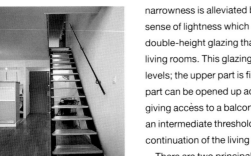

33

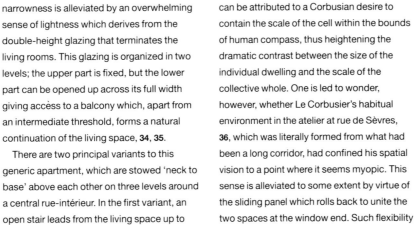

34   **35**

33 Charlotte Perriand worked closely with Le Corbusier on the development of the Unité's kitchens and was largely responsible for the detailed design of furniture, fixture and fittings throughout the apartments.

34, 35 Individual balconies form a natural extension of the living spaces; the glazed doors can be opened up across the whole width of the room.

36 Le Corbusier's corridor-like atelier at rue de Sèvres.

narrowness is alleviated by an overwhelming sense of lightness which derives from the double-height glazing that terminates the living rooms. This glazing is organized in two levels; the upper part is fixed, but the lower part can be opened up across its full width giving access to a balcony which, apart from an intermediate threshold, forms a natural continuation of the living space, **34, 35**.

There are two principal variants to this generic apartment, which are stowed 'neck to base' above each other on three levels around a central rue-intérieur. In the first variant, an open stair leads from the living space up to the parents' bedroom balcony above the kitchen and dining area. This balcony enjoys the same view out across the city as the living space below. It is equipped with fitted wardrobes and has its own bathroom, fitted with a bath, shower, wash basin and bidet. In the second variant, this arrangement is reversed, with the kitchen occupying the balcony, located in this case at entry level, which inevitably compromises the notion of the kitchen as a physical and symbolic focus.

The childrens' rooms are arranged in pairs and reached via a lobby with further cupboards for linen, storage and so forth. These long narrow spaces are just wide enough to accept a single bed apiece, and it is here that the apartments find their most cell-like expression. As at La Tourette, this sense of confinement

can be attributed to a Corbusian desire to contain the scale of the cell within the bounds of human compass, thus heightening the dramatic contrast between the size of the individual dwelling and the scale of the collective whole. One is led to wonder, however, whether Le Corbusier's habitual environment in the atelier at rue de Sèvres, **36**, which was literally formed from what had been a long corridor, had confined his spatial vision to a point where it seems myopic. This sense is alleviated to some extent by virtue of the sliding panel which rolls back to unite the two spaces at the window end. Such flexibility allows the two rooms to function as a single space, if preferred, or to share a common nursery or playroom, with its own balcony, where the children can play without disturbing their parents.

The notional integrity of each dwelling, the 'bottle' idea, is reinforced by Le Corbusier's adopted construction method. Each apartment is assembled independently within the reinforced-concrete armature and has its own sub-frame of steel joists which rest on lead pads to absorb vibration and prevent sound transmission through the structure. Party walls are made from independent timber-framed panels with a mineral wool backing. The degree of sound insulation and acoustic privacy achieved by this apparently primitive method is quite remarkable.

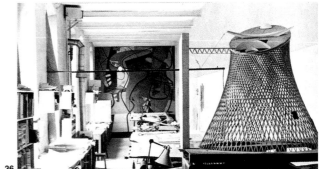

36

37 Massive *pilotis* define a shadowy base on which the mass of the Unité's 'hull' appears to rest.
38 The public concourse mid-way up the block provides a variety of communal facilities, including an hotel, shops and commercial offices.
39 The long public gallery on the western side of the block is reminiscent of the enclosed promenade deck of an ocean liner, directly reinforcing Le Corbusier's nautical metaphor.
40 Free-form 'smoke-stacks' and other items of cast-concrete nauticalia populate the Unité's roof deck floating high above the Mediterranean.

rues-intérieur (located on floors 2, 5, 7, 8, 10, 13 and 16) which continue the shadowy theme as a counterpoint to the revelatory lightness of the individual apartments.

The public concourse on levels 7 and 8 provides a 24 room hotel with restaurant and bar, shops and other facilities including a laundry, bakery, butcher, hairdressing salon, sauna, estate office and commercial offices, **38**. It is expressed at the northern end of both the long façades as an elongated glazed cut, like an enclosed promenade deck that terminates in the punctuation point of a free-standing escape stair, a heroically-scaled reminder of the Unité's free-plan, Domino ancestry. It is only at this point in the Unité that the double-height arrangement that characterizes the apartments is allowed to feature in the public domain; the long gallery on the western side of the block looks out to sea from behind vertical fin-like concrete baffles, reinforcing the nautical metaphor in a disarmingly direct way, **39**.

It is at roof level, however, that the Unité demonstrates its full architectural and metaphorical force. With its bridge-like gymnasium superstructure, its free-form 'smokestacks' (which emit satisfyingly

motor-like sounds) and its high parapet, which masks the surrounding urban development, the Unité's roofscape transports the visitor on a concrete deck floating high above the Mediterranean, **40**. One has to imagine the Bacchanalian party that took place here to celebrate the 1954 CIAM Conference, but one can see for oneself the children, sunbathers and joggers who regularly make use of the nursery school, pool, sundeck, gymnasium and 300 metre long running track: this is an illustration of the ship-board 'good life' par excellence.

Foundation and opposition

Standing on the roof deck more than forty years after the Unité's completion, amid signs of its continuing restoration, it is difficult to conceive of the problems that beset Le Corbusier and the ATBAT team during its construction.

It was on 13 October 1947, more than two years after Le Corbusier had first been given the Unité commission, that the foundation stone was laid. Those present at the ceremony included Le Corbusier, members of ATBAT, the contractor, Construction Moderne Française,

40

38

The extended dwelling

Implicit within Le Corbusier's notion of the Unité as a 'vertical garden city' is the ideal that its community should be socially self-supportive; it is this principle that is indicated by Le Corbusier's term 'logements prolongés', or extended dwellings. By 'extensions' he implied the collective mechanical services and social amenities, such as the nursery school, day-care centre, gymnasium and shops that contribute to, and complement, daily life in the individual unit.

The Marseilles Unité's community of approximately 1600 residents is served by communal facilities arranged on three principal public levels: on the ground, in the shopping 'street' halfway up the block and on the roof deck. Each of these elements finds clear formal expression.

At ground level are the massive *pilotis* that mark out a shadowy base on which the block appears to rest, **37**. Taking Le Corbusier's ocean liner metaphor to its limits, one can see these *pilotis* as supportive shores beneath the Unité's 'hull' as if it were waiting on the slipway in preparedness for its Mediterranean launch. Raising the block in this way assists its definition as a machine-like entity, subject to arcane systems of order and control; and entering the building, the resident is literally 'elevated' to his or her apartment. High-speed lifts disgorge onto subdued and artificially-lit

37

39

a departmental delegation headed by
M. G. Letourneau, by now the fifth post-war
Minister of Reconstruction, the Mayor Jean
Cristofol and a party of councillors from the
City of Marseilles.

Construction, **41–45**, was planned to last for
12 months but in fact lasted for five years and
came up against a series of difficulties
stemming variously from the poor organization
of the building site, the state's inexperience
in this kind of pilot housing scheme and
the unfavourable economic climate. The
assembly line anticipated by ATBAT, and
offered as a model for modern housing
construction, was to turn out to be little
more than empty rhetoric.

Despite the gradual rationalization of
the design which Le Corbusier and Bodianski
had achieved subsequent to the preliminary
scheme, the distance between theoretical
intention and the practical realities of
construction grew greater and greater.
Incompatibility between different kinds of
manufacture and production, difficulties in
assembling different materials, lack of control
of tolerances between in-situ components
and those made in the factory and shortages
of materials combined to create such delays

42

43

41

that the contractor was forced constantly to
interrupt building work: only the budget
soared skyward. Georges Candilis, who was
part of the ATBAT Unité team from 1946 to
1952 recalls the differences and frictions that
arose between Le Corbusier and Bodianscky
as the project ran into trouble. Their equally
strong, but markedly different personalities
drew them into a conflict which led ultimately
to Le Corbusier's withdrawal from ATBAT.
Candilis also testifies to the crucial role
played by Bodiansky: it was Le Corbusier
who 'spiritually conceived' the Unité, but it
was Bodiansky who was responsible for
its technical realization.[50]

Dependent as it was on the state for
administrative, technical and financial
direction, progress also suffered from the
combined effects of political instability and
opposition to the project itself. For example,
it had been planned to construct the building
in four phases, but in the summer of 1948,
faced with ever escalating costs, the
government proposed to limit construction
to the first, northern-most section only. But
Le Corbusier wrote furiously in the project's
defence and the Ministry relented.

Ultimately, however, credit for the fact that
the Unité was completed in the form which
Le Corbusier intended is due largely to
Eugene Claudius-Petit, who became the
project's sixth Minister of Reconstruction

in September 1948. He came forward as
its advocate each time Le Corbusier was
threatened, whether by institutions, because
of regulations, or by the various intrigues and
plots which were rife between 1947 and 1950.

Mud slinging

From the outset, opposition to the project
had come from every quarter. Like St Dié,
it was attacked in almost equal measure by
architects, planning and hygiene authorities,
conservatives, communists and the press.
Le Corbusier wrote bitterly: 'One campaign
followed another. I read the first article
to appear in the papers. What a headline!
"Protest by all but one of the architects of
the Morbihan against the project for a … etc.
… etc.". After that I decided not to read
another line about the Marseilles block.
I have kept my word, leaving it to the
poisonous little scribes to read their own
venomous outpourings'.[51]

Le Corbusier also noted wryly that the
mud on the site was less of a distraction
than the mud that was flung at the project
by its detractors. The first missiles came
at a meeting of the Conseil Supérieur de
l'Architecture et de l'Urbanisme de France, a
society of which Le Corbusier was a member:

'Between us – architects, engineers,
businessmen and myself – we had studied

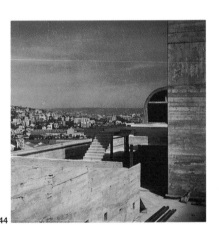

44

45

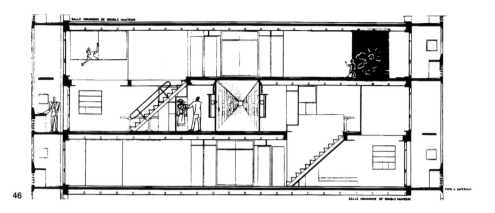

46 Sectional proposal for the unrealized Unité d'Habitation in Strasbourg, published in the *Oeuvre Complète*, 1946–52; the apartments are considerably smaller than those in Marseilles.
47 Perspective drawing of the Unité d'Habitation in Nantes-Rezé, published in the *Oeuvre Compléte*, 1946–52.
48 The Berlin Unité d'Habitation was compromised by the controls and regulations imposed by the city authorities to such a degree that Le Corbusier dissociated himself from the project before its completion.

approval any construction work considered to be of an experimental nature, and then promptly recognized the experimental status of the 'Unité d'Habitation Le Corbusier'.

More was to come: the architects of the SADA (Société des Architectes Diplômes par le Gouvernement) objected to the decision to allow the Unité to proceed outside of the building regulations: the Société pour l'Esthetique de France took legal action to have the site cleared; and in February 1950, when building work was practically complete, the President of the Ordre des Médecins de la Seine, himself a psychiatrist, declared that the unfortunate residents of the Unité would be driven mad by the noise created within it. According to him, the people of Marseilles had christened the project 'La Maison du Fada' – the lunatic asylum.[53] Ironically it is the pervading sense of peace and quietude that first impresses the visitor to the Unité's apartments.

Far from being daunted by such hostile publicity, however, Le Corbusier was expert at turning it to his own advantage. He also managed to make the best of the most difficult situations; it was due to the inordinately long construction period, for example, that he was able to organize so many tours and VIP visits to the site including those made by Alvar Aalto, Nicolas de Stael and Pablo Picasso. In 1949, members of the CIAM congress at Bergamo visited the first demonstration apartment on the third floor. When this apartment was opened to the public, the 'mud slingers' changed their aim: there was no more talk of slums. 'We asked for working-class flats', they whined, 'and here you are giving us flats for American millionaires'.[54]

Despite the Unité's apparent success, Le Corbusier knew long before its inauguration that the state was going to dissociate itself from the project. His proposal for the urbanization of Marseilles-Sud, prepared in 1951, which envisaged a further three Unités forming a quadripartite Cité Radieuse on Boulevard Michelet was stillborn. Furthermore, the government, wishing to draw a line under an experiment which had been criticized so often for being a bottomless financial pit, and lacking experience in the daily management of a block such as the Unité, decided to put all of the apartments on the market from 1952 onwards.

the project from every angle. Our arguments seemed irrefutable. We were opening a new chapter in welfare, and I awaited the spontaneous congratulations of my colleagues.

"A slum!" That was the first word spoken ... A report was sent to the Minister and we received a copy. It advocated the modification of our plans. The Minister summoned us and read the report.

"What do you think of it M. Le Corbusier?"
"I don't even consider it."
"Splendid", he answered. "From now on I propose to call the project the Unité d'Habitation Le Corbusier, and it will be referred to as such in all official documents. You are free of all restrictions and above the law. You are the judge of what you should do and can innovate to your heart's content. You alone are responsible"'.[52]

That conversation, if it is to be taken literally, was with the third Minister of Reconstruction. It was Claudius-Petit, however, who in October 1948 received, belatedly, the report of the Conseil Supérieur d'Hygiene Publique de France which advised him to halt construction of the project on the grounds that it violated the public health regulations. Unmoved, he deflected further regulatory difficulties by issuing a ministerial waiver in July 1949, exempting from building licence

In 1954, the Unité was constituted as a housing cooperative under a traditional French system of joint ownership. Designed from the outset to house middle-class residents, its community has not changed significantly since it was first occupied.

The Unité legacy

The Marseilles Unité was the first and largest single building of architectural importance to be completed in Europe after the war; and as Reyner Banham has observed, it was the first genuinely 'post-war' building in the sense that its innovative stance separated it definitively from modern architecture as practiced before 1939.[55]

The momentum of Le Corbusier's achievement at Marseilles carried him forward to plan Unités in Strasbourg, **46**, and Meaux and to build a further four: in Nantes-Rezé, 1953–55, **47**, Berlin, 1956–58, **48**, Briey-en-Forêt, 1957–61, **49**, and at Firminy-Vert. This last block, **50**, completed in 1968 after Le Corbusier's death, was commissioned in 1960 together with a church, youth centre and house of culture, by Claudius-Petit who was by then Mayor of Firminy. The history of these schemes is chequered, however: disputes

49

with the Berlin authorities led Le Corbusier to dissociate himself from the project before its completion; and the miserable budgets, lack of facilities, poor management and the slide into ghetto status which variously afflicted the remaining French Unités led to their decline in popularity and fall into disrepair.

Denied the Homeric landscape of southern France, and the brilliance of the Meditteranean sun, these buildings – all actually physically smaller than the Marseilles Unité – seem somehow further diminished. Uniquely in this group, the Marseilles block can still be seen as a magnificent conception. For Reyner Banham, at least, it represented one pinnacle of Le Corbusier's career, the building in which 'all the rhetorical consonances between modern technology and ancient architecture in *Vers une Architecture* most nearly come true'.[56]

It is to a phrase in that book that Banham also turned to define the moment of conception of the 'New Brutalism' which was to carry Le Corbusier's béton brut idiom forward internationally into developments such as the Alton West Estate in Roehampton, 1955–59, which transposed the message of St Dié into an English context, **51**. 'L'architecture', wrote Le Corbusier, 'c'est avec des matériels brutes etablir des rapports emouvements'. If any one building can exemplify this construction of moving

relationships from rough materials it is surely the Marseilles Unité.

It is exactly this quality that defined it the icon of the avant-garde generation of post-war architects for whom Brutalism became a vehicle to drive a path through the architectural establishment. 'Mies is great but Corb communicates', said Peter Smithson, who might be considered as the intellectual driver of this movement in England. The message that Le Corbusier communicated was, alas, lost in the translation as it worked its way through less able interpreters. The grim housing estates that pock-mark the fringes of our cities are debased and empty monuments to Le Corbusier's fundamental Humanism.

The demise of mass-housing projects such as Pruitt-Igoe in St Louis, Missouri, or Ronan Point, in the East End of London, has been spectacularized and noted as symbolic of a failure of the project of Modernism as a whole. But as one commentator has put it: 'To blame Le Corbusier for Ronan Point is like blaming Mozart for Muzak'.[57] And as the Brutalist generation slips into its dotage, and the mass-housing projects of that period are gradually being disregarded and demolished, the central message of Le Corbusier's Marseilles Unité is, for those of the current generation of architects willing to receive it, still refreshingly loud and clear.

49 The Unité d'Habitation in Briey-en-Forêt, seen in splendid isolation shortly after its completion.
50 The Unité d'Habitation in Firminy was completed after Le Corbusier's death.

Like the Unité at Briey-en-Forêt it is a much diminished inheritor of the Marseilles principle.
51 The Unité principle in an English context: the Alton West Estate in Roehampton.

50

51

Notes

1 Soltan, Jerzy, 'Working With Le Corbusier', in *Le Corbusier: The Garland Essays*, New York and London, 1987, p.1.

2 Le Corbusier, *Oeuvre Complète, 1938–46*, Zurich, p.16.

3 Le Corbusier, *Oeuvre Complète, 1946–52*, The Factory at St Dié, p.13.

4 ibid. p.13.

5 Curtis, William J.R., *Le Corbusier: Ideas and Forms*, London, 1992, Chapter 11, p.163.

6 Le Corbusier, *The Marseilles Block*, translated by Geoffrey Sainsbury, London, 1953, p.46. Le Corbusier continues: 'Unknown to me at the time, the Americans pounced on the Saint Dié plan and used it to demonstrate the rebirth of France. For years it was on exhibition, touring the towns of the USA and Canada'.

7 Le Corbusier, *Oeuvre Complète, 1938–46*, p.76.

8 Charlotte Perriand also escaped to Switzerland and joined the Resistance.

9 Essentially a regionalist movement, Syndicalism can be characterized as a synthesis of benign, laissez-faire capitalism and totalitarian communism. Its ideological touchstone was a faith in 'the plan' and the capability of intellectuals and industrialists to lead the advance of social and political progress. Le Corbusier became active in the movement during 1930, and edited the magazine *Plans* between 1931 and 1932.

10 Le Corbusier, *The Marseilles Block*, p.7.

11 Le Corbusier, *Oeuvre Complète, 1938–46*, p.94.

12 ibid. p.124.

13 This bald statement won Le Corbusier the approbation of the Marxist critic Andre Lurcat: 'So you insult the people by giving them a building that is 25 years out of date'. Quoted by Reyner Banham in 'La Maison des Hommes' and 'La Misère des Villes: Le Corbusier and the Architecture of Mass Housing' in *Le Corbusier: The Garland Essays*, New York and London, 1987.

14 'We used to have lunch in a little restaurant frequented by coachmen in the heart of Paris. It had a zinc-topped counter, and a kitchen at the back; half way up the space there was a balcony, and the front opened onto the street. One fine day we discovered it and realized that there were all the elements needed for an architectural mechanism corresponding to the organization of a house'. Le Corbusier, *Oeuvre Complète, 1910–29*, p.31.

15 ibid. pp.98–108.

16 ibid. pp.98 and 104. In French, Le Corbusier describes the typical inhabitant of the Immeubles Villas as 'un homme <de serie>' – literally, mass-produced man.

17 Le Corbusier, *Oeuvre Complète, 1910–29*, pp.78–86.

18 Le Corbusier, *The Marseilles Block*, p.10.

19 von Moos, Stanislaus, *Le Corbusier: Elements of a Synthesis*, Cambridge Mass. and London, 1979, p.51.

20 'The Chartreuse d'Ema near Florence made me conscious of the harmony which results from the interplay of individual and collective life when each reacts favourably upon the other. Individual and collectivity comprehended as fundamental dualism.' Le Corbusier, *The Marseilles Block*, p.45.

21 Le Corbusier, *Oeuvre Complète, 1910–29*, pp.34–39.

22 In *Vers une Architecture*, 1923, under the heading 'Eyes that do not See', Le Corbusier juxtaposes landmarks from the new machine age with great architectural monuments: 'a serious architect, possessing the eyes of an architect, will find in an ocean liner the first stage in the realization of a world organized according to the new spirit'; this section of the book is illustrated by pictures of liners culled from travel brochures. He was doubtless also aware of the Biblical resonances of the ship as 'ark', a symbol of salvation.

23 von Moos, op. cit., pp.150–151.

24 Le Corbusier, *The Marseilles Block*, p.22.

25 Le Corbusier, *Oeuvre Complète, 1929–34*, pp.66–71.

26 Curtis, op. cit., p.111.

27 Le Corbusier, *Oeuvre Complète, 1929–34*, in an essay entitled 'Un nouvel ordre de grandeur des elements urbains, une nouvelle unité d'habitation', pp.110–114.

28 Le Corbusier, *The Marseilles Block*, p.31.

29 This sectional arrangement can be traced further to Soviet social condensers of the 1920s, such as Ginzberg's Narkomfin building of 1928, with which Le Corbusier was familiar.

30 Le Corbusier, *L'Homme et l'Architecture*, Paris, 1947.

31 Other notable characters include Georges Candilis and the American Shadrach Woods who, together with Bodiansky, went on to form ATBAT-Afrique, Casablanca, 1951–55, and became founder members of Team Ten. The principal designers making up the ATBAT team were: Afonso, Andreini, Roger Aujame, Edith Aujame, Badel, Barnes, Candilis, Carellas, Chatzidakis, Creveaux, Doshi, Fenyo, Gardien, Gonzalez de Leon, Genton, Hanning, Hirvela, Hoesli, Kennedy, Kondracki, Kujawski, Lemco, De Looze, Maisonnier, Masson, Mazet, Nicolas, Perriand, Preveral, Provelongios, Rosenberg, Rottier, Sachinidis, Salmona, Samper, Seralta, Vaculik, Wogenscky, Woods, Xenakis, Yosisaka and Zalewski.

32 See Candilis, Georges, entry for Vladimir Bodiansky in *Contemporary Architects*, London, 1980, pp.102–103.

33 Le Corbusier, *Oeuvre Complète, 1938–46*, pp.172–173.

34 Le Corbusier, *Oeuvre Complète, 1929–34*, pp.74–89.

35 Le Corbusier, *Oeuvre Complète, 1338–46*, pp.174–189.

36 ibid. pp.80–89.

37 See Mackenzie, Christopher, 'Le Corbusier in the Sun', *Architectural Review*, February 1993, pp.71–74.

38 See Gans, Deborah, *The Le Corbusier Guide*, London, 1987, in an entry on the Marseilles Unité, pp.87–91.

39 Curtis, op. cit., p.164.

40 Wogenscky, André, in an essay entitled 'The Unité d'Habitation at Marseille', translated by Stephen Sartarelli, published in *Le Corbusier: The Garland Essays*, New York and London, 1987, p.125.

41 Banham, Reyner, *The New Brutalism*, London, 1966, p.16.

42 ibid. p.16.

43 Farmer, John, in an essay entitled 'Battered Bunkers', published in the *Architectural Review*, January 1987, p.63.

44 Scully, Vincent, *Modern Architecture: The Architecture of Democracy*, New York, 1961, p.45.

45 Le Corbusier, *Oeuvre Complète, 1938–46*, p.173.

46 Tropeano, Ruggero; Prouve's involvement in the project is explained in detail in an essay 'Unité d'Habitation de Marseille', published in *Le Corbusier, une encyclopedie*, Paris, 1987, pp.200–206.

47 Le Corbusier, *The Marseilles Block*, p.44.

48 See Tropeano, op. cit., pp.200–206.

49 Wogenscky, André, in an essay in *The Marseilles Block*, p.52.

50 Candilis, op. cit., p.103.

51 Le Corbusier, *The Marseilles Block*, p.8.

52 ibid. pp.9–10.

53 ibid. p.12.

54 ibid. p.46.

55 Banham, op. cit., p.16.

56 ibid. p.16; he continues: '...The Brutalist generation in Britain never tired of pointing out that the title given to the English translation – 'Towards a New Architecture' – falsified Le Corbusier's intentions ... Reading *Vers une Architecture* as a sacred text, they knew that it promised not a new architecture, but simply architecture as it always had been and always would be, as Le Corbusier believed the term had been understood by Perret, by Phidias, by Mansart or Michelangelo. Right or wrong, Le Corbusier had vouchsafed his younger readers a vision of a grandiose Mediterranean architectural tradition'.

57 Sam Webb, speaking on the 18th anniversary of the collapse of Ronan Point, 16 May 1986.

Right, the acrobatic forms of Modular man impressed in the shuttered concrete wall of the entrance hall. The foundation 'stone' is in the foreground.

Left, the Unité's brises-
soleil are arranged
in a crate-like pattern,
forming protective
loggias in front of
each apartment.

Right, the Unité as approached from the east from Boulevard Michelet and, opposite, as entered from the west.

Constructionally, the block combines in situ concrete elements with pre-cast components, often used as permanent shuttering, the whole composition deriving a giant, rusticated order.

Details of the main
entrance on the western
side of the block.

Right, seen here from the west, the public concourse mid-way up the block is described as if it were the promenade deck of a great ocean-going liner.

The double-height gallery on the western side of the block looks out to sea from behind thin vertical brises-soleil, reinforcing this space's ship-like qualities.

Right, individual
balconies form natural
extensions of the Unité's
living spaces; the glazed
doors can be folded
back to complete the
relationship. The
kitchens, designed in
close collaboration with
Charlotte Perriand, are
'little labour-saving
laboratories'.

It is at roof level that
the Unité demonstrates
its full architectural force;
its bridge-like super-
structure and free-form
'smoke-stacks' transport
the visitor on a concrete
deck floating high above
the Mediterranean.

A gentle ramp leads up to the roof-level crèche; the running track seen right, offers a 300 metre long route around the perimeter of the building.

The roof-level pool and
children's play areas are
thoughtfully placed and
appropriately scaled;
the rock-like forms in
the background appear
to echo the massive
mountain forms beyond.

Detail, left, of a concrete
staircase up to the base
of one of the ventilation
shafts and right, of the
curved concrete form
of the gymnasium
roof whose shape
is reminiscent of an
up-turned boat, its keel
line forming the ridge.

Site plan

1 pedestrian entrance
  from Boulevard
  Michelet
2 car entrance
  and exit
3 parking
4 main entrance
5 entrance hall
  and lifts

0   20 metres

0   60 feet

Drawings

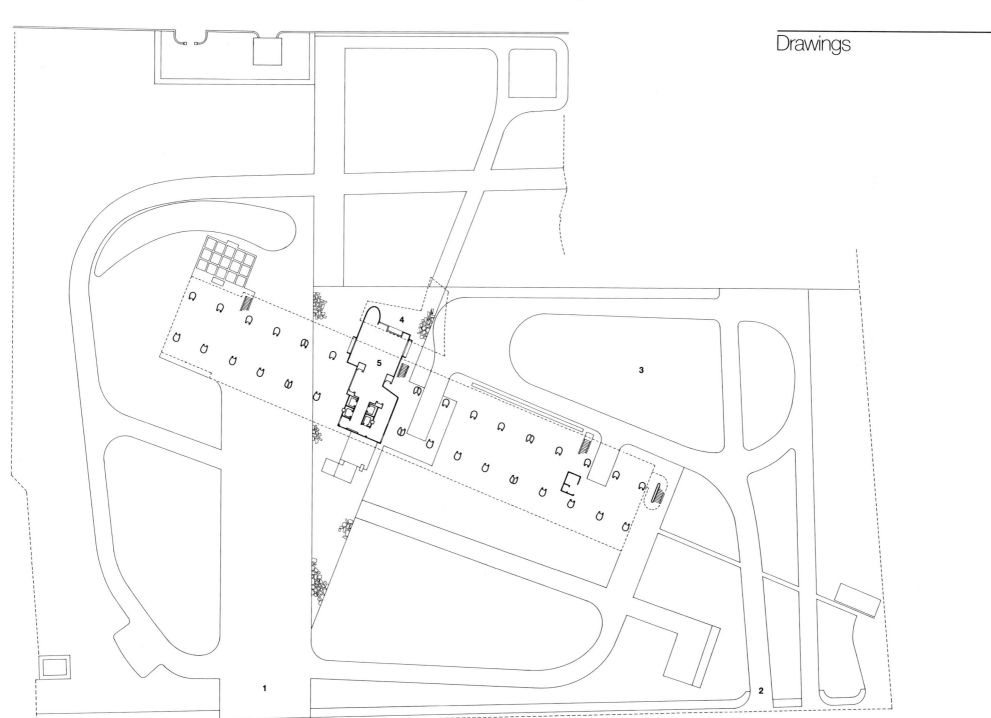

**Typical plan of floor
with interior street,
located on levels
2, 5, 10, 13 and 16**

1 duplex apartment
entered at terrace
level

2 duplex apartment
entered at gallery
level

3 escape stair

4 interior street

5 lift lobby

6 single aspect
duplex apartment

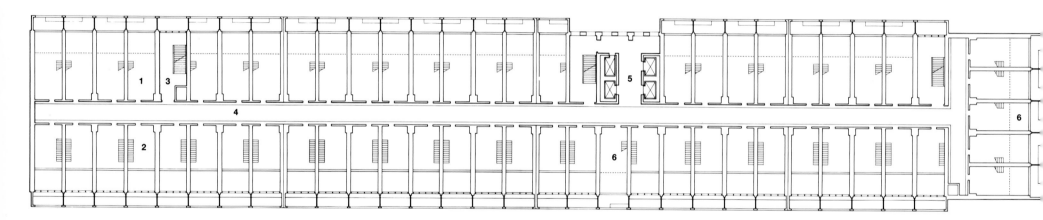

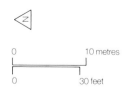

0   10 metres

0   30 feet

Plans of typical
duplex apartments
entered from levels
2, 5, 10, 13 and 16

1 interior street
2 entrance to
  apartment
3 kitchen
4 dining area and
  living room
5 dining area

and gallery
6 parents' bedroom
  with bathroom
7 children's bedrooms
8 balcony
9 void
10 parents' bedroom
  and living area
11 stowable ironing
  board
12 shower and wc

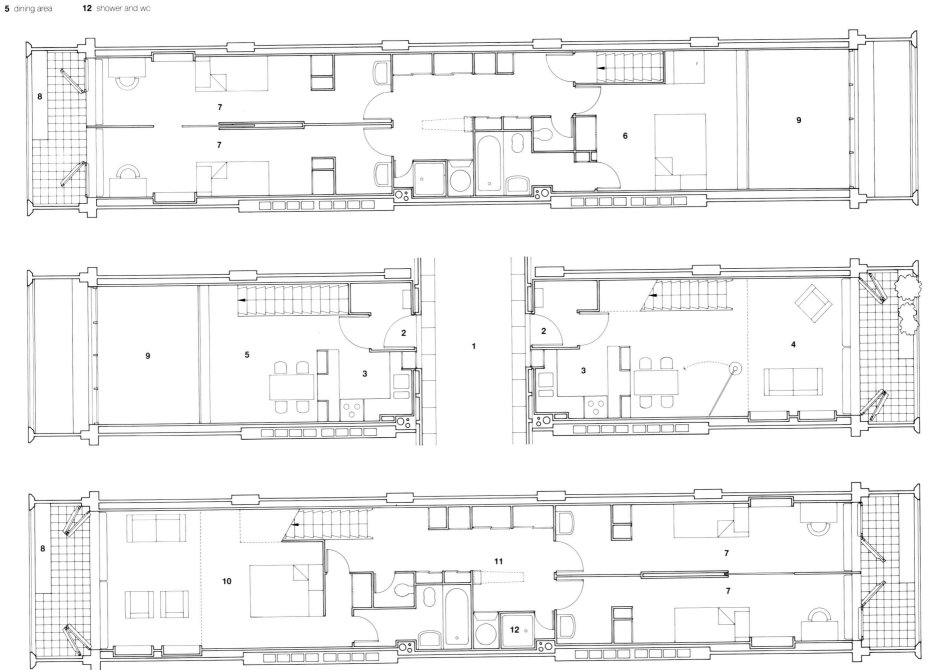

0   2 metres

0   6 feet

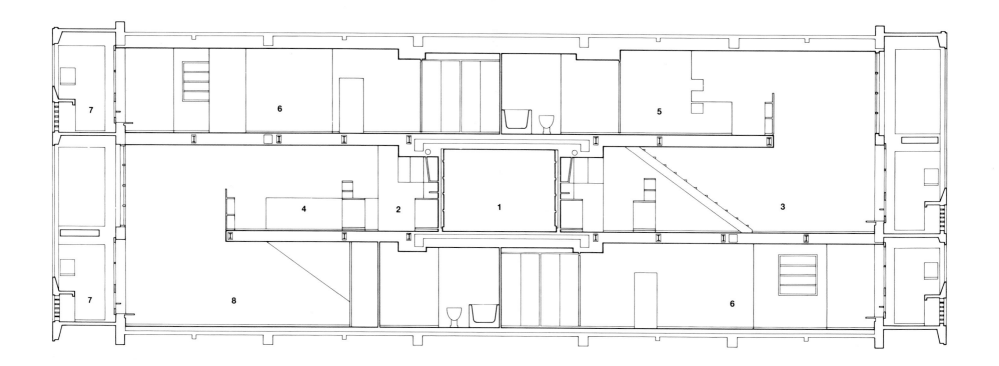

Section through typical duplex apartment

1 interior street
2 kitchen
3 dining area and living room
4 dining area

and gallery
5 parents' bedroom with bathroom
6 children's bedrooms
7 balcony terrace
8 parents' bedroom and living area

0   2 metres

0   6 feet

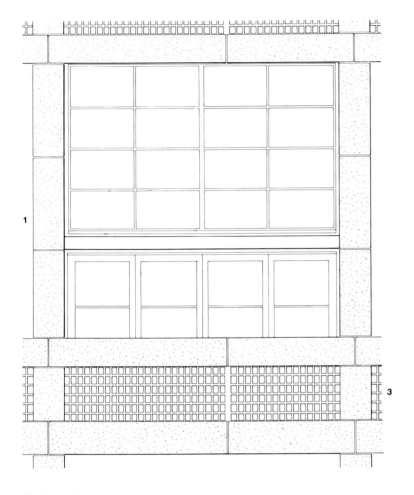
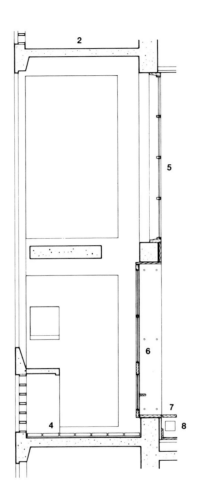
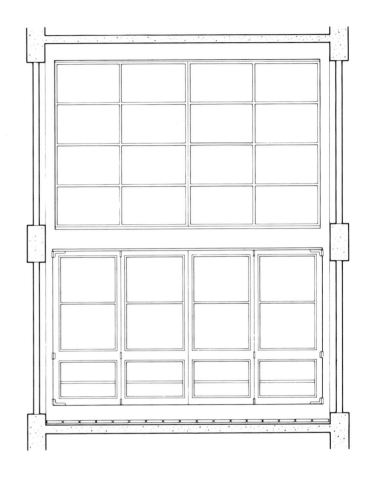

Detail elevations, section and plan of typical duplex apartment balcony

1 precast concrete facing panels as permanent shuttering

2 reinforced concrete in situ frame

3 precast concrete balustrade

4 concrete paving slabs

5 fixed glazing above door height

6 fully opening glazed doors to balcony

7 wooden bench seating above radiator

8 timber flooring

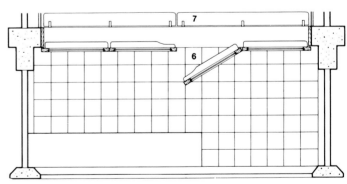

0   1 metre

0   3 feet

Plan at roof level

1 wind-breaker
  and stage for
  open-air theatre
2 ventilation stack
3 gymnasium
4 300 metre long
  running track
5 eastern solarium
6 upper terrace level
7 western solarium
8 balcony
9 lift tower
10 crèche
11 children's pool
12 children's play area
13 artificial 'mountains'

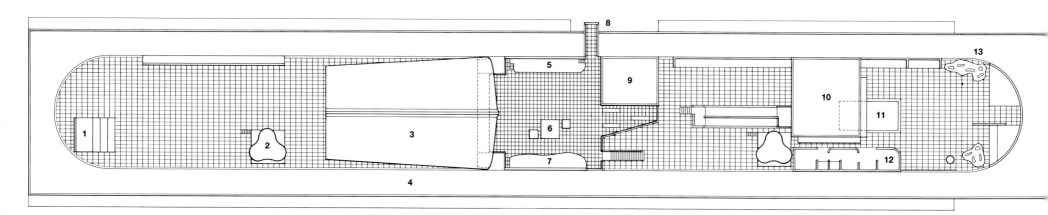

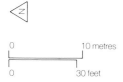

0   10 metres

0   30 feet

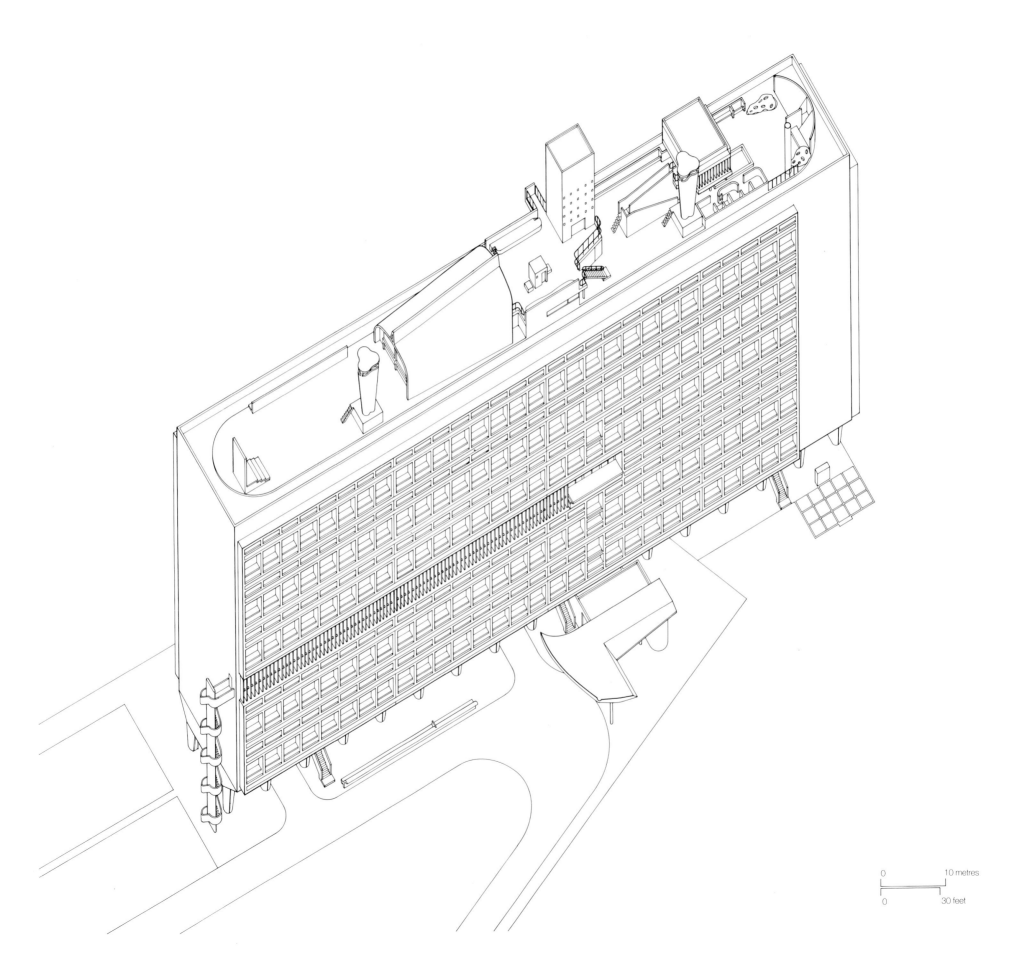

The Unité block
axonometric viewed
from the north-west

0   10 metres

0   30 feet

Structural section
illustrating Le Corbusier's
'bottle and wine bin'
principle of apartments
inserted within a
lattice frame

0   10 metres

0   30 feet

Statistics

Site area 3684 hectares, 8.65 acres

Building dimensions Length – 165m; depth – 24m; height – 56m to level of roof terrace

Cost Unknown

Total apartment floor area 28 773m²

Total usable floor area (excluding apartments, circulation and services) 5738m²

Total habitable floor area 34 518m²

General arrangement 19 floor levels served by seven internal 'street' levels

Apartments 337 separate family units of 23 different types ranging from apartments for single persons and couples without children to apartments for families with up to eight children

Apartment width 3.66m internally

Apartment height 4.8m floor to ceiling height in living area

Staircases Four public fire escapes, including one on the north-facing façade; one central spiral escape stair reserved for firemen

Lifts Three public lifts and one goods lift for public use: specification – load 1350 kg or 18 people, nominal speed 3.6 m/second. One goods lift for tradesmen's use only; specification – load 1000 kg, nominal speed 0.48 m/second

Central heating and hot water installation
Two underground oil-fired boilers, each of 1000 Kcal/hour, are served by three underground 60 000 litre fuel tanks. Warm air heating system served by eight heat exchangers and an electric generator located in the services void beneath the lower floor level. A 100m³ water tank is located at roof level. Heating is by forced air circulation, with partial air conditioning; air enters rooms through grilles at floor level along the window panes and exhausts in kitchens, bathrooms and wcs.

Waste disposal Via wet ducts in each apartment and two dry shutes on the landings of the north and south fire escapes. Kitchen sinks have double bowls, one of which discharges into a refuse chute

Amenities Entrance hall: concierge on 24 hour duty; Levels 7 & 8: 24-room hotel with restaurant and bar; shops and other communal facilities including a laundry, bakery, butcher, hairdressing salon, chemist, sauna, estate office and commercial offices

Roof terrace communal facilities including a gymnasium, nursery school, solarium, pool, open-air theatre and 300m long running track

Construction 36 reinforced concrete columns, each carrying 2000 tons, support a reinforced concrete 'lattice' frame into which separate apartments are built. Apartments have independent steel sub-frames isolated from the main structure on lead pads to prevent sound transmission. The outer beams of the main structure carry consoles for fixing balconies. Panels forming outer wall elements, brises-soleil and window linings are of pre-cast vibrated concrete with an exposed local white stone aggregate; fixing is by means of vibrated concrete brackets built into the framework. Individual apartment units are built of prefabricated standardized timber floor panels screwed to the metal subframe; the walls are timber framed and incorporate lead sheet to prevent sound travelling between dwellings.

Chronology

16 November 1944 M. Raoul Dautry is appointed as France's first Minister for Reconstruction and Urbanism

September 1945 Initiation of ISIA (apartements sans affectation individuelle) housing programme by the French state

November 1945 First project for a Unité d'Habitation on a site overlooking the old port of Marseilles at la Madraque, an area badly damaged by Nazi dynamiting and the allied landings in 1944 Area of site: 2650 hectares. Project provided 338 apartments in three blocks. Density: 600 inhabitants per hectare. Foundation of ATBAT (Atelier des batisseurs). Second project for a Unité d'Habitation on a site to the east of Boulevard Michelet.

26 January 1946 M. F. Billoux is appointed as France's second post-war Minister for Reconstruction and Urbanism

July–October 1946 Third project for a Unité d'Habitation on a site at Saint-Barnabe

22 January 1947 M. C. Tillon is appointed as France's third post-war Minister for Reconstruction and Urbanism

October 1946–February 1947 Final project for the Marseilles Unité d'Habitation on the actual site

March 1947 Commission confirmed following the submission of 170 project drawings

9 May 1947 M. G. Letourneau is appointed as France's fourth post-war Minister for Reconstruction and Urbanism

September 1947 Work begins on site

11 September 1947 M. Rene Coty is appointed as France's fifth post-war Minister for Reconstruction and Urbanism

14 October 1947 The first stone is laid

1948 Publication of *Le Modulor*

11 September 1948 M. E. Claudius-Petit is appointed as France's sixth post-war Minister for Reconstruction and Urbanism

June 1949 Construction of the shell is complete as far as the 8th floor. Model apartment is fitted out on the 3rd floor

25 July 1949 A ministerial waiver is granted, exempting from building licence approval for any construction work considered to be of an experimental nature

August 1949 Construction of the shell is complete up to roof level

8 August 1949 A ministerial order is issued recognizing the experimental nature of the project to construct the 'Unité d'Habitation Le Corbusier'

December 1949 Construction of the shell is completed in its entirety

25 August 1951 Official handover of the finished building

December 1951 Decision to sell the building to a residents cooperative

7 January 1952 M. E. Claudius-Petit resigns

14 October 1952 Official opening of the Marseilles Unité d'Habitation by M. E. Cluadius-Petit, Minister of Construction and Urbanism. Le Corbusier is made a 'Commandeur dans l'Ordre de la Legion d'Honneur'

14 January 1953 Foundation of the residents cooperative

2 December 1954 The residents cooperative holds its constitutive general assembly

1955 Completion of the Unité d'Habitation in Nantes-Rezé

1958 Completion of the Unité d'Habitation in Berlin

1961 Completion of the Unité d'Habitation in Briey-en-Foret

28 May 1963 The Unité d'Habitation park is given by the State to the City of Marseilles

26 October 1964 The Marseilles Unité d'Habitation façades and roofscape are scheduled under 'l'inventaire supplémentaire des Monuments Historiques'

27 August 1965 Le Corbusier dies at Roquebrune-Cap-Martin

1968 Completion of the Unité d'Habitation in Firminy-Vert

20 June 1986 The Marseilles Unité d'Habitation's public areas and common parts are added to the schedule of 'Monuments Historiques'

June 1987 Centenary of Le Corbusier's birth

1992 Celebration of the 40th anniversary of the Marseilles 'Cité Radieuse'. Restoration of the façades is completed

Select Bibliography

The following is a partial selection of the books in which the Unité d'Habitation is discussed or described

Banham, Reyner *The New Brutalism*, London, 1966. The definitive study of Le Corbusier's Brut idiom and its repercussions in the work of the post-war generation of architects who, for Banham, comprise the 'New Brutalists'. Banham posits Brutalism as a moral, as much as an aesthetic movement, and illustrates his argument with the work of architects and artists including Le Corbusier, Alison and Peter Smithson, James Stirling and James Gowan, Philip Johnson, Eduardo Paolozzi and Jackson Pollock, amongst others.

Besset, Maurice *Le Corbusier: To Live With the Light*, London, 1987. The chapter on 'Space and Plasticity' gives a concise critical insight into Le Corbusier's gradual transition from a Purist to a Brut idiom during the early 1930s. Besset also includes a comprehensive bibliography and chronology for all Le Corbusier's writings and buildings.

Brooks, H. Allen (ed.), *Le Corbusier: The Garland Essays*, New York and London, 1987. Contains several excellent essays on Le Corbusier's developing urbanism and the Marseilles Unité, including: Jerzy Soltan, 'Working with Le Corbusier'; Reyner Banham, 'La Maison des Hommes' and 'La Misère des Villes: Le Corbusier and the Architecture of Mass Housing'; André Wogenscky, 'The Unité d'Habitation at Marseilles'.

Curtis, William J.R. *Le Corbusier: Ideas and Forms*, second edition, London, 1992. Perhaps the best account of Le Corbusier's architectural and intellectual progress. Curtis defines Le Corbusier as a pivotal figure in the history of 20th-century architecture and places him in the context of a wider and older classical tradition. The Marseilles Unité is discussed in a chapter entitled 'The Modulor, Marseilles and the Mediterranean Myth'.

Gans, Deborah *The Le Corbusier Guide*, London, 1987. A concise guide to all Le Corbusier's built work worldwide, including information on the location and accessibility of the buildings.

Jencks, Charles *Le Corbusier and the Tragic View of Modern Architecture*, London, 1987. The Marseilles Unité and the development of Le Corbusier's Brutalist idiom are discussed under the heading 'Other Languages of Architecture 1946–65'.

Le Corbusier (Charles Edouard Jeanneret), *Concerning Town Planning*, London, 1947. The English translation by Clive Entwistle of *Propos d'Urbanisme*, first published in French in 1946.

Le Corbusier and de Pirrefeu, Francois *The Home of Man*, London, 1948. The English translation by Clive Entwistle and Gordon Holt of *La Maison des Hommes*, first published in French in 1942.

Le Corbusier *The Marseilles Block*, London, 1953; the English translation by Geoffrey Sainsbury of a text first published in French in 1950. Le Corbusier's proselytizing, polemical and, one suspects, slightly revisionist account of the Marseilles Unité, published to mark the building's completion. It also contains a straightforward description of the block and the individual apartments by André Wogenscky, the leader of the ATBAT design team.

Le Corbusier *Oeuvre Complète 1938–46*, Zurich, 1946. The early developmental schemes for the Marseilles Unité are illustrated on pp. 173–187.

Le Corbusier *Oeuvre Complète 1946–52*, Zurich, 1953. The Marseilles Unité d'Habitation is illustrated on pp. 189–223; the text includes Le Corbusier's address at the formal ceremony to hand over the building on 14 October 1952.

Le Corbusier *The Modulor*, London, 1954. The English translation by Peter de Francia and Anna Bostock of *Le Modulor*, first published in French in 1948.

Le Corbusier *Modulor 2*, London, 1958. The English translation by Peter de Francia and Anna Bostock of the French edition first published in 1955.

Le Corbusier *Le Poeme de l'angle droit*, Paris, 1955. An illustrated prose poem in which Le Corbusier draws out spiritual themes and obsessions concerned with the interplay of natural forces: earth and water, sun and moon, shadow and light, and weaves a sustaining myth around the notion of the 'harmonious solar day'.

Raeburn, Michael and Wilson, Victoria (eds), *Le Corbusier Architect of the Century*. Catalogue of the centenary exhibition held at the Hayward Gallery, London, 1987. Contains essays on Le Corbusier's approaches to urbanism and the development of the Unité principle including: Tim Benton, 'Urbanism, and The Sacred and the Search for Myths'; Judi Loach, 'Le Corbusier at Firminy-Vert'.

Serenyi, Peter (ed.), *Le Corbusier in Perspective*, New Jersey, 1975. Contains essays on the Marseilles Unité and Le Corbusier's use of the Modulor including: Peter Serenyi, 'Le Corbusier's Changing Attitude Towards Form'; Peter Collins, 'Modulor'; Rudolph Wittkower, 'Le Corbusier's Modulor'. Le Corbusier's reliance on early collective housing models and his fascination with monasticism is discussed by Serenyi in 'Le Corbusier, Fourier, and the Monastery of Ema'.

Sherwood, Roger *Modern Housing Prototypes*, Cambridge, Mass. and London, 1978. Includes a contextualized account of the Marseilles Unité and its impact on mass-housing typology.

von Moos, Stanislaus *Le Corbusier: Elements of a Synthesis*, Cambridge Mass. and London, 1979. Includes a lucid account of Le Corbusier's exploration of housing prototypes and the development of the Unité principle in chapters entitled 'Variations on a Utopian Theme' and 'Urbanism'.

Louis I. Kahn
Salk Institute
La Jolla 1959–65

James Steele

Photography
Peter Aprahamian; cover detail
also by Peter Aprahamian
Drawings
Ann Knudsen, John Hewitt

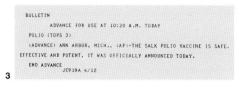

When discussing how he received the commission for the Salk Institute for Biological Research near La Jolla, California, Louis Kahn was fond of telling the story of Dr Jonas Salk's visit to his office in Philadelphia in 1959. After a preliminary discussion, Kahn took Salk on a tour of the Richards Medical Research Building at the University of Pennsylvania, **1**, and was asked how many square feet the building provided. The fact that it was comparable in size to the project that Salk envisioned seemed to impress his potential client, and was to be the most specific initial piece of programmatic information he was to receive. Kahn had actually come to Salk's attention through a friend who had heard the architect deliver a speech entitled 'Order for Science and Art', related to the Richards towers, and the noted scientist had only intended to contact him for suggestions of names of other architects he might interview. The two got on so well that Salk felt he need look no further, **2**, **3**.[1]

During their initial discussion, Kahn was also impressed by the fact that Salk wanted his laboratories to be the kind of place where 'Picasso could come to visit', and that medical research should not be confined to science alone. This image, of the humanization of science, and the possible unity of art and architecture struck a responsive chord in Kahn, for whom making the 'immeasurable measurable' continued to be a personal quest. As Kahn himself said, 'there was something else that he said which became the key to the entire space environment. Namely that medical research does not belong entirely to medicine or the physical sciences. It belongs to population. He meant that anyone with a mind in the humanities, in science, or in art could contribute to the mental environment of research, leading to discoveries in science. Without the restrictions of a dictatorial programme it became a rewarding experience to participate in the projection of an evolving programme of spaces without precedence'.[2]

In the first prospectus, produced by the Institute to generate capital for the new project, the far-sighted theme of health as a unitary, or holistic process is consistently stressed, as is the study of both the body and mind of the 'total person', **4**. To that end, it promotes a centre devoted to humane studies, and the inclusion of scholars in the belief that a study of 'a totality of values is integral to a vision of total health'.[3] The choice of the initial faculty of the Institute, which consisted of a distinguished group of resident and non-resident fellows working under Jonas Salk as President and Director, reflect this belief, **5**. In alphabetical order, these were Jacob Bronowski, Melvin Cohn, Francis Crick, Renato Dulbecco, Edwin Lennox, Jacques Monod, Leslie Orgel, Les Szilard and Warren Weaver. Implicit in this selection, particularly of the mathematician and humanist Bronowski, who contributed so much to the understanding of the place that science should occupy in modern culture, was a new attitude towards biological research, in which the humanities were not only seen to have a part, but in which physics and chemistry, traditionally seen as distinctly different studies, were now considered to be merged.[4]

Three distinct phases
Early in 1960 Kahn visited La Jolla to help Salk determine how much land would be required for the project, and the City Council voted to contribute the site to the Institute in the spring of that year.[5] The first scheme was presented by Kahn in conjunction with the formal

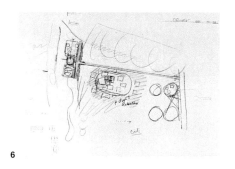

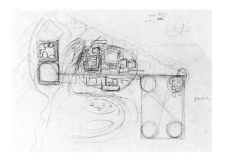

announcement of the project by Salk on March 15, 1960.[6] The residual influence of the Richards Medical Building is still evident, with the laboratories shown as clusters of towers near Torrey Pines Road. An intermediate zone, flanking the deep ravine that bisects the site is set aside for houses, designated as 'the Living Place', for the fellows on the south, and a recreation centre on the north. The 'Meeting Place', far out on the bluff overlooking the Pacific, is shown as having a narrow straight access road and a bridge of its own, and is rendered as a linear grouping positioned parallel to the face of the cliff. In it, lecture halls and an auditorium are organized around enclosed courts, all sharing an elongated ambulatory, intended to bring the scientists together, **6**, **7**. In a second version, which appeared nearly a year later, the vertical laboratory towers were replaced by four rectilinear, two-storey blocks set perpendicular to the sea. These are joined by a service area which completely separates them from the parking area and Torrey Pines Road, to the west. The central courts, around which each pair of laboratories are organized, were the result of Dr Salk's having mentioned his love of the monastery of St Francis of Assisi to Kahn, and a letter from the architect to Professor W.H. Jordy in August 1960, in which he mentions his intention to revisit the monastery himself, lends credence to its importance as the source of this idea, **8**.[7]

In their second configuration of 1961–62 the laboratories are made up of four clear span spaces, made possible by five box girders running across each rectangle, with a 'V'-shaped folded plate system perpendicular to the girders, spanning between them, **10–13**. Piping, threaded through the folded plates, is channelled into the box girders, to towers on the outside edge of each set of

7

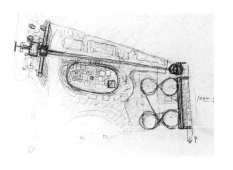

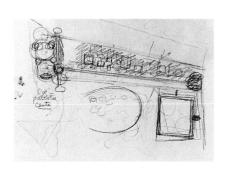

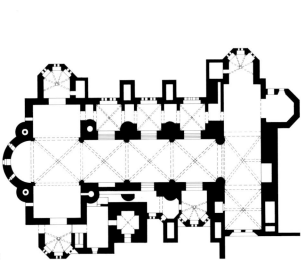

8

9 The cliff-side site chosen by Salk and Kahn has spectacular views of the Pacific.

10–12 Kahn's second scheme was based on two sets of laboratory blocks, each enclosing a planted, rectilinear central court, with both the Meeting Place and residences for the fellows adapted more closely to the contours of the cliff.

13 Salk and Kahn discussing the second scheme.

14 The American Consulate in Luanda was also an influential, environmental model for the Institute design.

15 Hadrian's Villa, in Tivoli, inspired Kahn to 'wrap ruins' around the Meeting Place.

16, 17 The Meeting Place, in its final configuration, was organized around a square, central hall.

18 A central, pedestrian street, broken into small-scale segments by stairs between levels, was intended to serve as a spine for the residential group.

9

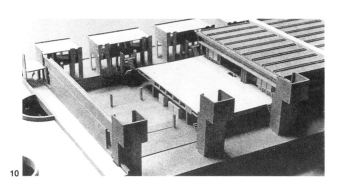

10

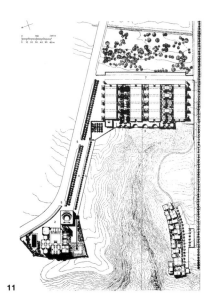

11

12

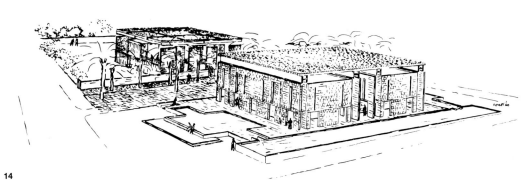

14

13

16

laboratories, used for exhaust. By turning the vertical duct shafts of the Richards Medical Building on their side, Kahn, the city architect not accustomed to such a large site, was beginning to respond to the expansiveness of the area available to him, as well as to pragmatic problems of dust on pipes which he had faced in the Research facility in Philadelphia. In addition to providing a relatively dust-free pipe chase, the folded plate system also allowed light to enter through the roof, as indicated in study models which show monitors punctured through the upper most set of Vs. The inequity, of allowing light into the top floor and not the bottom level of each two-storey laboratory block, because the second interior system could not be penetrated as well, may have been a factor in Kahn's agreeing to scrap the box girder and folded plate combination later on. The virtual inaccessibility of the pipes, and the need to have them make a 45 degree turn to run through the box girders to reach the exhaust towers, was the main reason given for the change.

In addition to the revision of the laboratories, the design of the Meeting Place in this scheme represents a significant departure for Kahn, as an extension of his 'theory of walls', first attempted in the American Consulate in Luanda, Angola, **14**, to counteract heat and glare. At a time when the main technological problem being addressed by modernism was how to make a glass curtain wall section thinner, Kahn was thinking about the space between the inner and outer surface and the possibility of separating the two. As he said: 'In the Salk project ... I am developing walls around buildings to take care of the glare. I do not think that venetian blinds and other kinds of window devices are architectural. They are department-store stuff and don't belong to architecture. The architect must find an

architecture out of glare, out of the wind, from which these shapes and dimensions are derived. And these glare walls are based on a very simple principle which I got... when I was in Africa. These walls I'm developing for the Salk Center in San Diego are in recognition of this discovery of the law of light'.[8]

Derived from Hadrian's Villa in Tivoli, **15**, the spaces in the second version of the Meeting Place, which include an auditorium, library, dining room and gymnasium, as well as guest quarters, are grouped around a covered hall, which is the ambulatory of the original scheme turned inward into a square, **16–18**.

The final scheme

After contracts were signed in the spring of 1962, Salk requested that Kahn simplify both the configuration of the laboratories, from four rectangular blocks to two, and the folded plate system which he felt was too inflexible.[9] Kahn concurred in the need for a reduction in the number of laboratories, but had hesitations about changing the structure writing that 'he felt the loss of the folded plate construction'.[10] The basic ideas of the 1961–62 scheme, of scientists' studies placed away from the laboratories in a central garden, and auxiliary spaces forming vertical towers on their external wall remained the same, but the architect increased the number of floors to three, with one of these below ground level. The five box girders spanning the width of the laboratories, and the 'V'-shaped folded plates running perpendicular to them, were replaced with thirteen Vierendeel beams, which create a 9 ft high service space above each of the three floors, allowing pipe chases to be dropped to the 65 x 245 ft floor below with more latitude than before. Mechanical

17

18

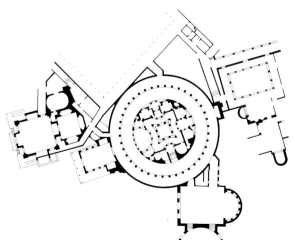

15

19

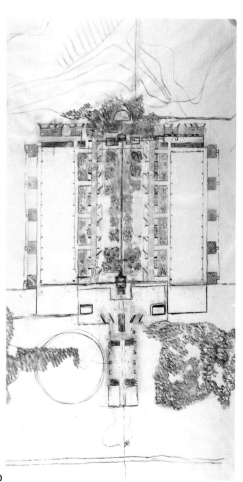

20

rooms at the northern end of each rectangular block, and an extension for offices, overlooking the Pacific were also refined, but remain essentially the same as in the earlier plan, **19, 20**. The study towers, which now give the courtyard its distinctive, serrated edges, are called 'porticos of studies' in the final working drawings, indicating the architect's and client's intention that they serve as the arcade of the 'cloister' they both envisioned. These studies, which are grouped into pairs, align with the mechanical rather than laboratory floor levels, and are separated from them by bridges, in order to maintain a sufficient physical and psychological distance between the two. Each laboratory block has five study towers, with each tower containing four offices, except for those near the entrance to the court, which only contain two. A diagonal wall allows each of the thirty-six scientists using the studies to have a view of the Pacific, and every study is fitted with a combination of operable sliding and fixed glass panels in teak wood frames. The differentiation used in these windows, which is similar to that in the Esherick House in Chestnut Hill, is typical of Kahn, who believed that the purpose of fenestration should be clarified with the part used for natural light separated from grills for ventilation, **21–23**.

Another important change that took place in the design involved the central court, which Kahn had always visualized as a lush garden. By the time of substantial completion of the laboratories and studies in 1965, the architect had still not determined what form it should take, and after seeing an exhibit of Luis Barragan's work at the Museum of Modern Art in New York in that same year, Kahn wrote to him, with an offer to collaborate on the court. Barragan came to the Institute early in 1966, and as he later recalled, told Kahn at first

sight of the muddy field between the laboratories, 'Don't put one leaf nor plant, not one flower, nor dirt. Absolutely nothing – and I told him, a plaza... will unite the two buildings, and at the end, you will see the line of the sea. Lou was thinking, and stated a very important thing – that the surface is a façade that rises to the sky and unites the two as if everything had been hollowed out', **24, 25**.[11]

Dr Salk was not with the two when Barragan first shared this realization with Kahn, joining them a bit later in the court. He recalls that this idea was enthusiastically presented to him by both men, but that he felt some misgivings when Barragan described his cloister as a 'plaza for all nations', since he wanted it to be private.[12] The commissioning of landscape architect Lawrence Halprin, from San Francisco, in the late summer of 1966 indicates that these misgivings extended beyond metaphor, but Kahn eventually rejected additional embellishment, implementing Barragan's idea in the middle of 1967.[13]

In its final configuration, the Meeting Place seems to be the reciprocal of the laboratories, gaining in spontaneity what they have lost. In contrast to the second phase scheme, which is mostly rectilinear, with the exception of several semi-circular apses and redoubts, the third is a careful balance between the rational and the organic in which each element occupies its appropriate place in a thoughtful composition. The square theatre of the earlier plan has been replaced by a classical, fan-shaped proscenium, cut into the cliff, which introduces visitors to the complex. The square central hall, however, which diagrams the form necessary for meeting, remains, as does its open external equivalent overlooking the Pacific. The series of spaces surrounding the inner hall transform from cubes and towers on its northern and eastern edge, to circles in squares

21

22

23

19, 20 Following a directive from Salk to simplify the second scheme, Kahn reduced the four laboratory blocks to two, flanking a single, central court.

21–23 Studies for the scientists provide places to escape from the concentrated routine of laboratory work; each has shuttered windows giving direct views to the Pacific.

24, 25 Kahn's continual struggle to determine the correct character of the central court was finally resolved by Barragan, who advised that it be free of landscaping.

24

25

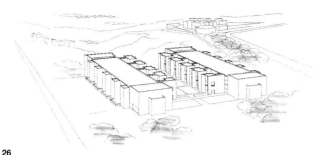

26

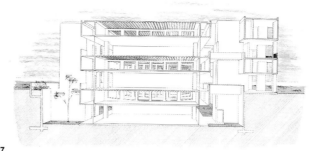

27

28

and squares in circles on the west and south, in a delightful volumetric translation of leeward and windward, sun and shadow, land and sea, with the plan resembling a diurnal freeze-frame diagram of a tree reacting to the light.

Little attention has thus far been given to the Living Place in the final scheme for the Institute, located directly across the ravine from the Meeting Place, to the north. In it, residences of various sizes were designed for research staff, scholarship holders and visitors in units that range from houses to apartments, as well as overnight accommodation and common areas. These are all placed on both sides of a central walkway, with parking provided on the exterior, southern edge. The residences step down on four levels of equal length as the internal street approaches the Pacific, breaking down the impression of distance, and giving the entire complex the intimate scale of a small village, **26–28**. A loop in the contours of the ravine closer to the laboratories would seem to have been a more desirable location for direct access and a more compact massing of residences, and when asked about this Kahn once again raised the important issue of distance, which had already proven to be so vexing in establishing the location of the studies. Answering a question with a question he responded by asking: 'How far is too far, how near is too near?' in typical Socratic fashion.[14] This sense of a retreat far enough away from the main place of work, which had also governed the choice of the position of the Meeting Place, was the main factor in the choice of the location of the residences, and views up and down the coast was another. As described by Brownlee and DeLong: 'In the third version of the houses for fellows, revised for the last time during the early months of 1962, seven different types

of two-storey buildings equipped with ample porches and balconies lined both sides of a narrow pedestrian street. Together they could accommodate more than fifty residents and guests. At either end, two-bedroom houses shared small plazas with adjacent guest quarters – the larger and more spacious of these was located at the western edge overlooking the ocean'.[15]

The possible realization of the Living Place at this point is even more problematic and unlikely than that of its meeting component, opposite. Speculative housing at this edge of the property has now completely changed the character of this part of the site, so that the ocean views of the southern half of the complex are now blocked, and the spirit of the concept has been compromised.

In their final detailing and materials, the laboratories, as built, reflect the architect's careful concern, evident in the design of all parts of the Institute.

Concrete

In determining the mix to be used in the concrete, which is the major material of the laboratory complex, and also intended to be used in the Living and Meeting Places, Kahn researched the components used in Roman pozzolana, in order to achieve a similar, reddish hue. He paid close attention to the forms, which were made of ¾ in exterior plywood, filled and sanded, and finished with coats of catalysed polyurethane resin. These were able to be used as many as eight times before being repaired and refinished.[16]

Rather than try to hide the joints between the panels, which would have resulted in some spalling, Kahn decided to accentuate them, chamfering the edges to produce a V-shaped groove at these

29

26–28 The studies, on which Kahn lavished much care, are located directly across from the interstitial mechanical space, rather than the laboratories, in order to provide more privacy. **29** Dr Salk readily attributes the choice of site, with its dramatic juxtaposition of sea and sky, to Kahn. **30–33** Due to the close interrelationship between building and ground, a great deal of excavation was required during construction.

31

30

32

33

34–36 Salk shared Kahn's enthusiasm for exposed concrete and became involved in the final approval process, checking colour and detailing of subterranean walls prior to the placement of those above them.

37 Structural diagram illustrating the principle of post-tensioning the columns; tension bars similar to those in the columns are also threaded through the bottom chord of each of the trusses to provide earthquake resistance.

34

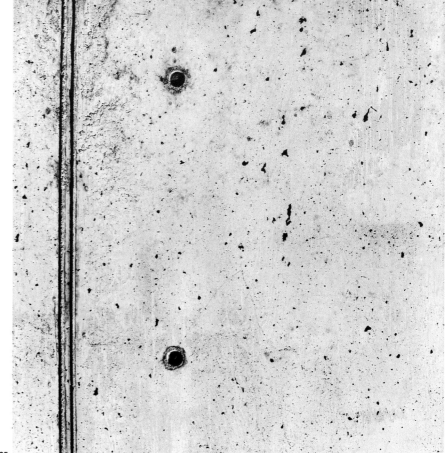

35

points along the wall surface, **34**. To avoid leakage and bleeding, the contractor used solid corners and gasketed joints between sets of gauged forms.[17] The conical holes left by the form ties were also not patched, so their spacing was carefully considered, and they were filled by a lead plug, hammered tightly into each to prevent corrosion of the steel ties, **35**.

Dr Salk was particularly interested in the colour and quality of the concrete and became involved in the approval of test walls, which would eventually form retaining walls, which would be covered with fill and not be visible. He, along with Kahn, rejected several batches before the final mix was accepted, **36**.

Structure

Stringent seismic criteria related to construction in the San Diego area made it difficult for Kahn's structural engineer, August E. Komendant, to convince local building officials, who wanted him to use a steel frame, that a concrete, Vierendeel truss system would have the required flexibility. They agreed only after Komendant had submitted a report containing over 400 pages of doubly integrated deflection computations that demonstrated that post-tensioned columns would provide the main resistance to lateral seismic forces. These columns, which absorb both dead and live load compression plus vertical post-tensioning forces, have been designed to maintain zero tension if subjected to lateral movements of the kind delivered by earthquakes. The vertical ends of the 9 foot deep trusses, which are spaced 20 feet on centre and have a clear span of 65 feet, alternate with the columns to form the integral, vertical support of the building. The stress steel bars, which were progressively post-tensioned against wedge anchor plates at the top of each truss as construction proceeded, were coated with asphalt paint and inserted in metal conduit to prevent bonding with the concrete. Three of these bars, similarly painted and encased, are draped through the bottom chord of each of the 18 foot wide trusses, acting like elastic 'tendons' that will elongate if an earthquake should occur, **37**. In this way, Komendant was able to provide a building which has twice the amount of controlled ductility of a steel structure of comparable size.[18]

As described in issues of *Engineering News-Record* released while construction was still under way: 'The trusses' bottom chords are post-tensioned, with the tendons slightly draped through the end panels to help resist the reaction shear. Unlike the column tendons, the truss tendons are grouted in their flexible steel conduits. The top chord of the vertical web members are reinforced. Each truss was cast in two sections, with a construction joint at the top plane of the bottom chords. Since the bottom-chord concrete merely serves as a protective cover for the post-tensioning cables, the cross section of the bottom chord is much shallower, and thus more flexible than the top chord, which must resist compressive forces with a combination of concrete and reinforcing steel... thus resulted the requirement for a monolithic casting of the web members of the top chord'.[19]

Building services

The sophistication of the mechanical systems is in keeping with the general philosophy of flexibility and reliability applied by Kahn in the design of the building itself. A high-temperature water system was

36

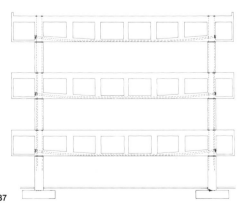

37

38 As might be expected in a building requiring such careful environmental control, the HVAC systems are very complex. **39** Final installation of the shutters for the studies.

40, 41 Kahn freely admitted his dislike of exposed pipes; his provision of large mechanical spaces between the laboratory floors allows them to be hidden.

39

chosen instead of steam as the main energy source for the central plant of the Institute. By submitting hot water to a pressure of 200psi, it *can* be heated to 350ºF without flashing to vapour, allowing for high levels of energy without the maintenance problems that usually accompany steam systems. High-temperature water is produced in the plant by a combination of natural gas-fired boilers, plus jacket water heat and exhaust gas heat from cogeneration engines. The heated water is then distributed to various building systems where it discharges its energy to produce space heating, space cooling, domestic hot water and steam for laboratory sterilizers, in a simple, low-maintenance energy system derived from a central source. Redundancy, which gives every mechanical system enough capacity for one on-line unit, with one on stand-by, gives service staff the ability to perform routine maintenance on almost all plant equipment without interrupting service.

Because research activity goes on all day, the heating, ventilating and air-conditioning systems must also remain in operation constantly. Ventilation is required to be 100% fresh air since the potential hazards of the laboratory environment prohibit re-circulation. The minimum number of air changes per hour is twelve. The North Building utilizes a 'dual duct system' for its heating and cooling. Two separate supply air ducts have been installed. One is heated with a central re-heat coil, while the other is cooled with a central chilled water coil to between 55 and 60ºF. Local zoned thermostats then regulate mechanical dampers which mix the hot and cold air supplied to each zone to maintain required room temperatures. The South Building uses a different heating and cooling design, called a 're-heat system', in which only a cold air

duct, cooled by a central chilled water coil, is necessary. The chilled water used to cool both the north and south cold air ducts is generated in absorption-type chilling units which operate on a chemical cycle, as opposed to a mechanical or Freon-type cycle. A 233 ton absorber is sufficient most of the year, but during the hot summer months, one or both 750 ton absorbers are used.

The electrical service, provided by three separate power sources, guarantees a reliable supply to the Institute. The normal source is the local utility company circuit 245 which enters the Institute from the north. An alternative is circuit 65, entering from the south. A third power service, which is synchronized with these two utility circuits, is an in-house co-generation plant, which has two 650KW units driven by 940 HP reciprocating engines. These are capable of meeting base requirements but utility power must be used to supplement their output at periods of peak demand during the working-day. By generating most of its own electrical power, the Institute has not only greatly reduced its utility bills, but has also reduced the possibility of a sustained power outage, which would threaten vital work in progress. As added insurance against this, there are two small emergency generators which are set to start up automatically if there is a power shortage. There are additional systems, necessary to a research laboratory, which have been provided, such as a 2000 gallon-per-day reverse osmosis system that provides high-quality distilled water to each laboratory sink. After reverse osmosis, the water is sent through charcoal filters and resin polishing bottles to purify it further, before it is held in stainless steel storage tanks. It is then pumped through a closed-loop circulating system, to prevent it from stagnation before being

tapped at laboratory outlets. Compressed air, used in laboratory incubators, is provided by two reciprocating compressors that send it through an after-cooler to remove condensed moisture before it passes through a second stage of air-drying in a refrigeration-type dryer. This dried, compressed air is then delivered at 40psi through the interstitial space piping to its point of use in the laboratories. Steam is also needed for sterilization purposes. It is produced via two steam generators from energy available in the high temperature hot water loop. After it is used for sterilization, the steam condenses, and the condensate is pumped back to the central plant, where it is either recycled into the steam generators once again, or dumped into drains, depending on its water quality. Natural gas, diesel fuel, liquefied carbon dioxide and special gases are also available for use by researchers, completing the list of services to the laboratories, **38**.[20]

It is useful to describe these systems in detail not just because the complex function of the project suggests it, but also because the thoughtful provisions made for them belie Kahn's general reputation, in some quarters, as an impractical dreamer, who frequently overlooked such details. While he was undoubtedly assisted by a very talented team of consultants, the decision to shift from a folded plate to Vierendeel structure was ultimately his alone. As he said, in connection with the University of Pennsylvania Medical Laboratories: 'I do not like ducts; I do not like pipes. I hate them really thoroughly, but because I hate them so thoroughly, I feel they have to be given their place. If I just hated them and took no care, I think they would invade the building and completely destroy it. I want to correct any notion you may have that I am in love with that kind of thing', **40, 41**.[21]

38

40

41

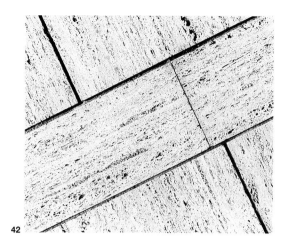

42

Critical evaluation

Louis Kahn embodied the critical method in both practice and teaching, to the extent that he had one full-time member of staff available for discussions on the progress of each of his projects at all times. He encouraged objective analysis and would welcome, rather than be offended by, relevant evaluations that have been made in the three decades since the completion of an institute generally regarded as his masterpiece. The most consistent, and positive part of that commentary has been the value of the foresight shown in making allowances for flexibility and change in the laboratories in an integral, rather than superficial way, through the provision of 'interstitial' spaces for mechanical services, **44**. While considered by some to be financially and spatially excessive when built, these have proven to be viable, repaying their original cost many times over.

Equivalent to this in a more general sense was Kahn's distinction between 'form' and 'design', which differed from the general understanding of these terms. As Marshall Meyers, who worked with him has explained: 'He talked about "design" and "form" often. To him design was the "how" and form was the "what". Design was those things which were personal, which were his: the colours he liked, his love of natural materials, his preference for certain proportions and shapes. Form was what to do. He searched for realizations which, if found, would belong to everyone'.[22]

Form, for Kahn, also had an 'existence will', and the architect's role was to allow it to manifest itself with as little hindrance as possible, so that personality, technique and trend would not dominate. The 'realizations' that Marshall Meyers speaks of were those that were fundamental to human nature, to the extent of even being above the cultural differences which design should answer to. The materials used in the Salk project, then, while expressive of such a search, are a function of choice, and have proven to be especially prescient, setting this project outside the usual considerations of style and fashion to which others are constantly exposed.

Kahn frequently spoke of a 'timeless' architecture, and of discovering 'what has always been, and what will always be'. His diverse historical interests, from Roman engineering techniques to Scottish castles, were all related to this idea of enduring institutions and durable transcendent forms that were above whim and fancy. His concrete here has a pozzolana additive not only intended to soften its appearance, but to make a symbolic connection through time to the origins of this composite material. Slate, which was the first choice for the central courtyard because of its striking contrast with the concrete, and its ability to convey the sombre dimension of an institution engaged in a constant struggle against life-threatening diseases, was eliminated because of cost, and replaced with travertine, which has similar symbolic connections. Because of its relative softness, the travertine has not lasted as well as the slate may have over time, but has proven to be a perfect visual and tactile foil to the concrete walls. Teak, used as latticework screening in the scientists' studies facing into the court, was similarly believed to be financially excessive by many at first, but in a subtle detail characteristic of this architect, was left unvarnished, to weather naturally, further reducing maintenance. Each decision in the design, made in this way, has ensured longevity in an endeavour increasingly fraught with the risk of renovation or demolition, **42**, **43**.

The Institute has fared equally well in broad considerations of function, with the exception of its main entrance and the clarity of circulation throughout. In a critique written shortly after the completion of the complex, Stanford Anderson was one of the first to note that, in the radical change that occurred between the first and last schemes, Kahn's original intention of having a 'non-hierarchical, semi-continuous series of units stretched across the site, translating between the private domain of the dwellings and the public and ideologically central meeting house' was lost.[23] Implied in that loss was the impossibility of any scientist now simply being more than 'the first among equals' in a community of scholars engaged in a common pursuit. The symmetry of the final design, which has resulted from several very plausible concerns expressed by Dr Salk, about the inherent possibility of competition between people working in different sets of buildings each centred around their own courtyard, as well as undue cost, which was accepted by Kahn as having greater clarity, was nonetheless imposed upon his original form realization and has changed it.

As Anderson has said: 'The approach from the east presents the visitor with the hard and bleak symmetry of the monumental stairs and the (from this view) windowless concrete buildings. Since the central feature of this symmetry is a void, the visitor is neither positively received nor is it possible ...to know which way to turn. The sense of an impending wrong decision is intensified by the over split in the site which becomes more emphatic as one

43

44

45

46–48 One frequently heard criticism of the design is the lack of a clear public entrance and circulation system, or reception area, which is now difficult for visitors to locate, as well as the absence of suitable conference rooms, due to the fact that the Meeting Place has yet to be built.

49 The Assembly Building in Bangladesh, which was Kahn's final project, represents the culmination of many of the ideas first used in the Salk Institute.

looks west...'.[24] In Anderson's view, the obvious expedient of a closure across the eastern end of the laboratories would be equally unsatisfactory because it defeats the sense of continuity along the north–south axis that was always Kahn's intention, and irrevocably establishes this hierarchical, bilateral condition as a constant.[25]

The preparation, over a seven-year period, of such a scheme by a California office, and its imminent construction have made this a particularly sensitive and controversial question, confirming its importance as an unresolved issue. On the other hand, there is a powerful impression conveyed by the open front door of the Institute, as finally realized, that can only be compared to the discovery of a hidden ruin, where the line of demarcation between building and nature is clearly drawn. As in Ostia or Phaesilis, where a single extended footstep is the only measure between a forest floor cushioned with pine needles and a paved Decumanus lined with partially recognizable structures on either side, the move upward through a small wood onto the central court of the Institute is as deliberately elemental as the architecture itself, the certitude of a conventional 'reception hall' replaced with a sense of anticipation and discovery now rare in an increasingly sterilized and predictable world, **46**.

There is, finally, the constant awareness that this is an incomplete dream, missing its most vital component. The Meeting Place, on which Kahn lavished so much love, and which he saw as the antithesis of the laboratories, and an irreplaceable component of the entire project, has never been realized, halted by Dr Salk on the pretext of design 'premise', rather than lack of funds, which

was the real reason. It was to be the embodiment of the ideal of unity expressed in the original mission statement of the Institute. While the residential portion of the complex may arguably have been omitted without serious damage to the form idea, the loss of the Meeting Place has seriously compromised it, to the great detriment of the institution. This loss is felt at several levels, most poignantly in the lack of any communal space except for a reception area, **47**, and auditorium, **48**, in the South Building which might begin to approximate to such a function in the laboratories. The expansive talent of Jacob Bronowski, for whom the Meeting Place would have been the perfect mileau in which to discuss the cultural implications of science, was wasted within the one-dimensional restrictions of the laboratory, where research, not philosophy, is the main priority, and others, with his broad perspective, have not followed him. Another level of the realization of loss is historical, in that an important stage in Kahn's intellectual evolution, regarding the space existing inside structure, bracketed as it has been by the Embassy in Luanda and the Assembly Building in Bangladesh, **49**, has not been physically transcribed. Dr Salk still maintains that the Meeting Place may yet be built, but since attention and financial resources have now been focused on the construction of a reception hall at the opposite end of the site, the probability of this happening seems increasingly remote.

Kahn's legacy

If the laboratories may be referred to as the lungs of the Salk Institute, the Meeting Place was to be its brain, and the body is incomplete. It was not a direct request of the client, but a desire inferred by a

47

48

49

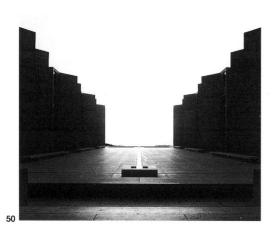

50

particularly intuitive architect from every word and gesture he was able to respond to, including the final configuration of the site itself. As Kahn once said: 'Need stands for what is already present, and it becomes a kind of measurement of the already present. Desire becomes a sense of the not yet made. That is the main difference between need and desire ... the architectural programme that comes to you then, becomes transformed, because you see the needs in it, and you see that which has not been expressed in the inspirations you feel. The society of spaces talking to each other in a plan is what reveals itself as an architectural validity, a harmony discovered out of the mere areas in a programme'.[26] Without the Meeting Place, the harmony evident in Kahn's final plan regrettably remains unfulfilled.

After Kahn's death in 1975, there was a great deal of speculation about his place in history, which, at this remove, now seems secure. The part played by the Salk Institute in establishing that place, in both concept and realization is substantial, because it marks a point of integration irrespective of questions related to translation of form. Ironically the exploration of internal, structural space, which is indicated so clearly in the layering between the inside and outside walls of the Meeting Place was soon to be redirected into an identifiable style which, at its best, retained something of the joyfulness contained in Kahn's contemporary translation of the Maritime Theatre, but at its worst was a vehicle for impermanent facadisim, at the opposite extreme to his eternal architecture. At the height of its popularity, Michael Graves, who did as much as Robert

Venturi and Charles Moore in promoting it, said that: 'If we should regard one figure as responsible for the turn of events that we are now experiencing in architecture as a move away from the modern movement, it would have to be Louis Kahn. Certainly there were and are documents such as "Complexity and Contradiction" that bring us to a conscious level of understanding of the breadth of things that were being missed by modern architecture in the academic sense, but in terms of the work alone, Lou was the first to say, wait a minute, that isn't the only answer ... we've been struggling with this idea of technology for so long now of making the walls thinner and thinner, lets look at it a different way. In a way what many people are doing now – whatever we call it – would not have taken the same route if it hadn't been for Lou's work... In the stylistic sense I don't think that's true. I don't think that he is very influential today'.[27]

The subsequent failure of post-modernism to establish a durable, perpetuating language, is precisely *why* Kahn's influence was not discernible in the style, and the recent renewal of interest in his work, particularly among students who have grown weary of trying to decipher charts that purport to trace all of the variants that have followed since, is indicative of his ability to rise above style. Students crowded into lecture halls to listen to this diminutive, charismatic man, who spoke in a poetry they could only partially understand, because they had finally discovered someone who spoke about order, permanence and timelessness. Such things are rarely discussed in schools today, but the students' desire to talk about them remains strong, especially at a time when the belief in institutions is fading.

The international mixture of students in Kahn's Masters class at the University of Pennsylvania, under the leadership of Dean G. Holmes Perkins, who had been given a mandate in 1951 to expand the curriculum of the School to include the totality of the man-made and natural environment, ensured the dissemination of graduates with a more contextual view toward architecture, who took these ideas back to their respective countries. While widely touted as a principle of post-modernism, the perfect fit between building and place, seen in such examples as Stirling's Staatsgalerie in Stuttgart, is very rare, and yet contextualism, or 'Critical Regionalism' as Kenneth Frampton calls it, has survived the death of the style, emerging now with localized agendas of its own.

Kahn discussed his work at length in his design studio, and since the Salk Institute occupied him for six years, from 1959 to 1965, it, along with the Assembly Hall in Bangladesh, and the Indian Institute of Management in Ahmedabad, had an enormous influence on a large number of students. They absorbed the lessons that each had to offer, especially about adaptation to site, climate and culture. Poised as it is at the juncture of land, sea and sky, the La Jolla project strikes a responsive chord in the American psyche as a calliper of the furthest extent of western expansion, on its precipice above the Pacific. Like the early Missions in this region, it acknowledges the need for closure in a windswept landscape, compromised by the open axis from east to west. The cloisters of those Missions, as well as their massive walls and deep-set, shuttered windows, were a response to nearly continuous sunshine which, while mostly benign, in combination with ocean breezes, is deceptively strong, with a high degree of glare. Kahn was absorbed with the question of the meaning of light, which here is ambivalently presented as both the source of life and the means of its destruction. The story of the evolution of the laboratories is one of both simplification and reduction, with the central courtyard transformed from a microcosmic paradisaical garden, as it is in the Alhambra, into a horizontal, reflective façade, open to the sky. His choice of materials, on the other hand, takes the harmful effects of light, as well as the corrosive action of salt air into consideration, since each is the most durable and yet vital option possible for its expressed purpose.

Kahn often attempted to describe the creative instinct through reference to its genetic source, frequently using a bilateral diagram, in which the words 'Silence and Light' were written on either side of a central, axial line. The primal necessity of light is implicit in this reduction, and he insisted that it be considered a generating force in all of his architecture. The Salk Institute changes in aspect during each hour of the day, depending on solar angle and the shadows that are cast, but is most memorable at sunset, when the horizon becomes a fiery wall at the end of the court. For this last hour it is the physical embodiment of Kahn's diagram, the closest he has ever come to realizing 'chapter zero' in any of his work, fully allowing for all of the new discoveries that have followed.

51

Notes

1 David B. Brownlee and David G. DeLong, *Louis I. Kahn: In the Realm of Architecture*, New York, p.330.

2 Louis Kahn, *Writings, Lectures, Interviews*, New York, 1991, p.118.

3 Salk Institute Prospectus, 1959, p.8.

4 Statement by Dr Warren Weaver delivered at the Biltmore-Hotel, New York, May 6 1963.

5 Brownlee and DeLong, op. cit., p.330.

6 ibid. p.330.

7 Heinz Ronner and Sharad Shaveir, *Louis I. Kahn: Complete Works 1935–1974*, Boston, 1967, p.133.

8 Kahn, op. cit., p.150.

9 Ronner and Shaveir, op. cit., p.141.

10 Kahn, op. cit., p.207.

11 Brownlee and DeLong, op. cit., p.441.

12 Jonas Salk's address to the ACSA Technology Conference in San Diego, 1992.

13 Brownlee and DeLong, op. cit., p.441.

14 Louis Kahn's lecture to the Masters class, University of Pennsylvania, 1969.

15 Brownlee and DeLong, op. cit., p.444.

16 Salk Institute public relations brochure, p.3.

17 ibid. p.4.

18 Technical Bulletin Stress Steel Corporation, August 1966, Bulletin No. 21, p.1.

19 *Engineering News-Record*, January 27 1966, p.6.

20 Salk Institute public relations brochure, p.10.

21 Richard Saul Wurman and Eugene Feldman (eds) *The Notebooks and Drawings of Louis I. Kahn*, Philadelphia, 1962.

22 *Architecture and Urbanism: Louis I. Kahn: Conception and Meaning*, A+U Publishing, 1983, p.224.

23 Stanford Anderson, 'Louis I. Kahn in the 1960s', *Boston Society of Architects Journal*, 1, 1967, p.27.

24 ibid. p.28.

25 ibid. p.29.

26 John Cook and Heinrich Klotz, *Conversations with Architects*, New York, 1973, p.180.

27 *A+U*, op. cit., p.220.

Specifications

Date of completion: July 1965

Dimension of each laboratory: 245ft (length) x 65ft (width)

Laboratory ceiling height: 11ft

Height of interstitial space: 9ft

Number and spacing of Vierendeels: 13 per building at 20ft centres

Dimension of courtyard: 270ft x 90ft

Size of light wells: 40ft x 25ft

Aluminium service slots: 4ft 8in (length) x 10ft (width) @ 5ft O.C.

Total gross square footage including all auxiliary structures: 411,580 sq ft

Structural Engineer: August E. Komendant

Structural Consultant: Ferver Dorland and Associates, Associated Structural Engineers, San Diego, CA

Laboratory Design Consultants: Early L. Walls Associates, La Jolla, CA

Site Engineer: Rick Engineers Co., San Diego, CA

Landscaping: Roland S. Hoyt, San Diego, CA

Landscape Consultant: Luis Barragan, Mexico City, Mexico

General Contractor: George A. Fuller Co., New York City

Mechanical and Electrical: University Mechanical and Engineering Contractors Inc., San Diego, CA; Fred S. Dubin Associates, New York City; Capital Electric Co., San Diego, CA

Job Captain for Louis Kahn: Jack MacAllister

Courtyard paving: travertine marble

Metalwork: A242 steel

Bibliography

'Academic ratrace', *Architectural Review*, 139, March 1966, pp.168–9.

'Address by Louis I. Kahn; April 5, 1966', *Boston Society of Architects Journal*, 1967, pp.7–20.

Anderson, Stanford, 'Louis I. Kahn in the 1960s', *Boston Society of Architects Journal*, 1, 1967, pp.21–30.

Andrews, Wayne, *Architecture in America*, New York, 1977, p.161.

Borck, F.K., 'Planung mit Installationsgeschossen Dargestellt an Bauten des Cesundheitswesens in Usa and Kanada', *Bauwelt*, 64, June 18 1963, p.1033.

Frampton, Kenneth, *Modern Architecture: A Critical History*, Cambridge and New York, 1980, pp.244–6.

Guirgola, Romaldo, *Louis I. Kahn*, Boulder, Colorado, 1975, pp.60, 66–75.

Hall, Mary Harrington, 'Gifts from the sea and the high hopes of Jonas Salk', *San Diego Magazine*, 14 February 1962, pp.41–5, 105–6.

Hammett, Ralph Warner, *Architecture in the United States: A Survey of Architectural Styles Since 1776*, New York, p.306.

Harms, Hans H., 'Trends in Architektur: USA-Louis I. Kahn', *Bauwelt*, 54, October 28 1963, pp.1252–61.

Hughes, Robert, 'Building with spent light', *Time*, January 15 1973, pp.60–65.

Hughes, Robert, 'Brick is stingy, concrete is generous: Salk Institute', *Horizon*, 16, Autumn 1974, pp.36–7.

Jencks, Charles, *Modern Movements in Architecture*, Garden City, New York, 1973, pp.213–33.

'Jonas Salk: der Sinn des Menschen fur Ordnung', *Werk*, July 1974.

Jordy, William H., 'Symbolic essence of modern European architecture of the twenties and its continuing influence', *Society of Architectural Historians*, 22 October 1963, pp.186–7.

Kahn, Louis, I., 'Form and Design', *Architectural Design*, April 1961, pp.152–4.

Kahn, Louis, I., *The Notebooks and Drawings of Louis Kahn*, edited and designed by Richard Saul Wurman and Eugene Feldman, Philadelphia, 1962, pp.48–61.

Kahn, Louis, I., 'Remarks', *Perspecta*, 9/10, 1965, pp.332–5.

Kahn, Louis, I., *Drawings*, Los Angeles, 1981, pp.27–32.

'Kahn not for the faint-hearted', *AIA Journal*, 55, June 1971, pp.28–9.

Komendant, August E., *18 Years with Architect Louis I. Kahn*, Englewood, New York, 1975, pp.41–73.

'Laboratory 1: precession of massive forms', *Architectural Forum*, 122, May 1965, pp.36–45.

'Labs Slab', *Architectural Review*, 143, March 1968, pp.173–4.

Lobell, John, *Between Silence and Light*, Boulder, Colorado, 1979, pp.7, 25, 34, 76–85.

'Louis I. Kahn exhibit', *Arts and Architecture*, 82, July 1965, pp.36–7.

'Louis I. Kahn; Oeuvres 1963–1969', *Architecture d'Aujourd'hui*, 142, February–March 1969, pp.80–87, 100.

'Louis Kahn', *Architecture d'Aujourd'hui*, 33, December 1962, pp.29–34.

'Louis Kahn: en Ameridansk Arkitekt', *Arkitekten*, 8, August 1966, pp.149–60.

'Louis Kahn: Institut Salk', *Architecture d'Aujourd'hui*, January 1967, pp.4–10.

Maki, Fumihiko, 'Kahn, Louis, I., Richards Medical Research Building, Pennsylvania 1961, Salk Institute for Biological Studies, California, 1965'. Edited and photographed by Yukio Futagawa. *Global Architecture*, 5, 1971, pp.9–25.

McCoy, Esther, 'Buildings in the United States: 1966–1967', *Lotus*, 4, 1967–8, pp.50–57.

McCoy, Esther, 'Dr. Salk talks about his Institute', *Architectural Forum*, 127, December 1967, pp.27–35.

Magnago Lampugnani, Vittorio, *Architecture of the 20th Century in Drawings*, New York, 1982, p.162.

Mee, Charles L., 'Louis Kahn', *Three Centuries of Notable American Architects* (ed. Joseph H. Thorndike), New York, 1981, pp.288–9, 292, 294.

'The mind of Louis Kahn', *Architectural Forum*, 127, July–August 1972, pp.42, 45, 85–87.

Nairn, Janet, 'Conference dissects works of five very different architects', *Architecture*, 73, October 1984, pp.16, 18, 21.

'An old master's footnote preserves an early idea', *Fortune*, 74, July 1966, p.126.

Pierson, William Harvey, *American Buildings and Their Architects: The Impact of European Modernism in the Mid-Twentieth Century*, Vol 4, Garden City, New York, 1972, pp.383–7, 389–90, 411–12.

Ragon, Michel, 'Power of Doubt', *Connaissance des Arts*, December 1980, pp.84–91.

Ronner, Heinz, *Louis I. Kahn: Complete Works, 1935–74*, Boulder, Colorado, 1977, pp.143–67.

Roth, Leland M., *A Concise History of American Architecture*, 1979, pp.301–3.

Roth, Ueli, 'Zwei Forschungslabratorian', *Werk*, 54, April 1967, pp.193–204.

Rowan, Jan C., 'Wanting to be; the Philadelphia School', *Progressive Architecture*, April 1961, pp.142–9.

'Il Salk Institute di Louis Kahn', *Architettura*, 11, November 1965, pp.462–3.

'Salk Institute for Biological Studies', *Architecture + Urbanism*, January 1973, pp.28–9, 61, 79–88.

'Salk Institute for Biological Studies, La Jolla (San Diego)', *Werk*, July 1974, pp.804–5.

'Salk Institute, La Jolla', *World Architecture*, 4, 1967, pp.40–47.

Scully, Vincent, *Louis I. Kahn*, New York, 1962, p.36.

Scully, Vincent, 'Light, form and power, new work of Louis Kahn', *Architectural Forum*, 121, August–September 1964, p.166.

Scully, Vincent, 'Recent works by Louis Kahn', *Zodiac*, 17, 1967, pp.80–103.

Scully, Vincent, *American Architecture and Urbanism*, New York, 1969, pp.221–2.

Smith, G.E. Kidder, *A Pictorial History of Architecture in America*, New York, 1976, pp.818–19.

Smith, G.E. Kidder, *The Architecture of the United States*, Garden City, New York, 1981, pp.94–7.

Stern, Robert A.M., *New Directions in American Architecture*, New York, 1969, pp.19–21. Revised 1977.

Temko, Allan, 'Evaluation: Louis Kahn's Salk Institute after a dozen years; what it is and what it might have been', *AIA Journal*, 66, March 1977, pp.42–9.

'Ten buildings that point to the future', *Fortune*, 72, December 1965, pp.174–5, 178.

Tentori, Francesco, 'Il passato come un amico', *Casabella*, 275, May 1963, pp.34–40.

Tyng, Alexandra, *Beginnings: Louis I. Kahn's Philosophy of Architecture*, New York, 1984, pp.40–43, 74–5, 140–42, 147–8, 165.

'Ulkomaat', *Arkkitehti*, February 1974, p.23.

Weeks, John, 'A design approach' in *Design for Research; Principles of Laboratory Architecture* (ed. Susan Braybooke), pp.4–8.

West, Don, 'Doctor Salk's bold new venture', *Pagent Magazine*, February 1962, pp.156–61.

Whiffen, Marcus, *American Architecture, 1606–1976*, Cambridge, Mass., 1981, pp.426–33.

Wilson, Richard Guy, 'Gold Medal for 1971; Louis Isadore Kahn', in *The AIA Gold Medal*, New York, 1984, pp.123, 212.

Previous spread,
the entrance from
Torrey Pines Road.
Below and opposite,
the unobstructed view
of the Pacific from the
entrance is one of the
most memorable
impressions that the
laboratories convey.

A line of water beginning
at the entrance and
running the entire
length of the courtyard,
culminates in a fountain
at its western end,
symbolic of the
Pacific nearby.

The projecting studies, like the cloister of a monastery, cast deep shadows into an arcade. Following spread, diagonal elements projecting out from the studies were a specific request of Dr Salk, who wanted each scientist to have a view of the ocean.

Employing very
straightforward means,
Kahn has provided
seemingly infinite
juxtapositions of forms
that are a constant
source of delight.

Durable materials have
ensured the longevity
of the complex in such
harsh climatic conditions.

The travertine paving in
the central court is also
used on stair treads.

Below left, exterior
view of the library.
Right, Kahn saw the
studies as 'the place
of the oak table and
the fireplace', where the
routine of the laboratory
could be momentarily
left behind.

The Salk Institute is the
embodiment of Kahn's
idea of silence and light.

Site plan

(prior to final revision)

1 laboratory group 1
and central court

2 laboratory group 2
and central court

3 holding pen

4 residences for
fellows and visitors

5 residence parking

6 meeting place

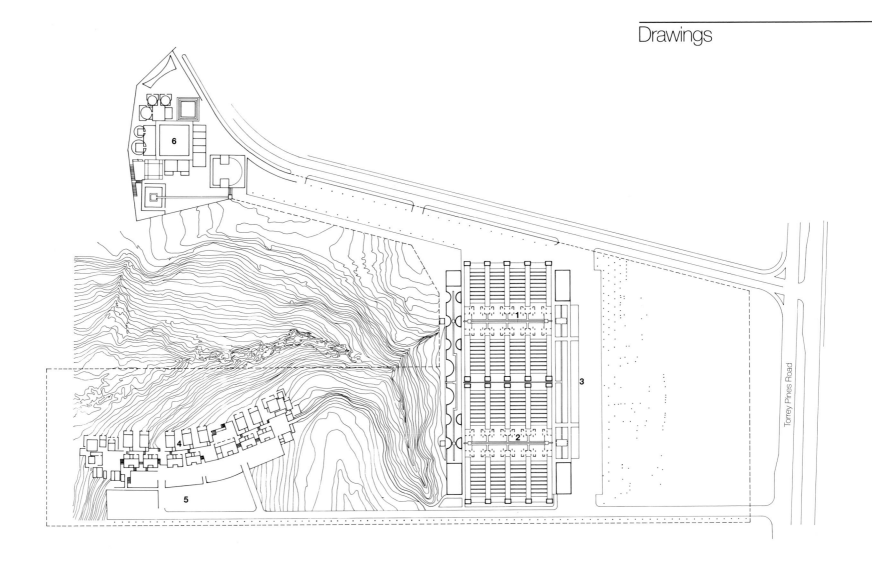

Torrey Pines Road

0   100 metres

0   100 yards

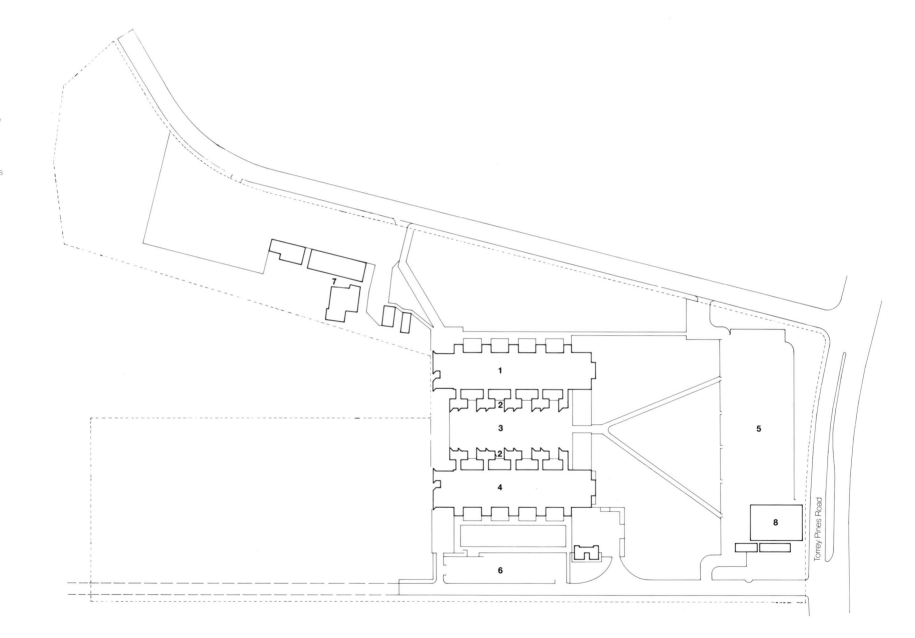

0   100 metres

0   100 yards

Lower floor plan

at laboratory level

1 laboratory
2 garden
3 office
4 mechanical room
5 incinerator
6 hot and cold
   air supply
7 electrical room

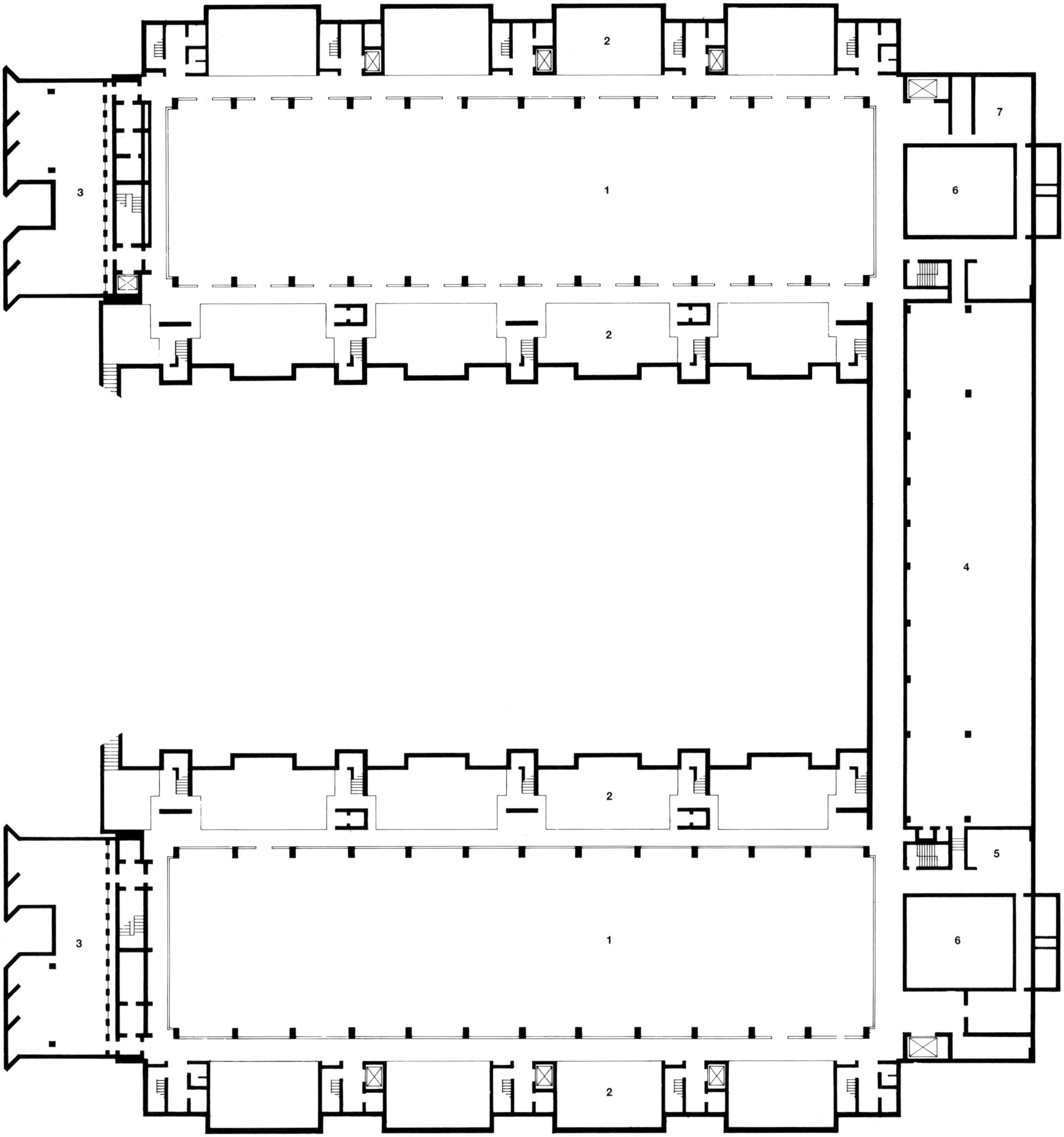

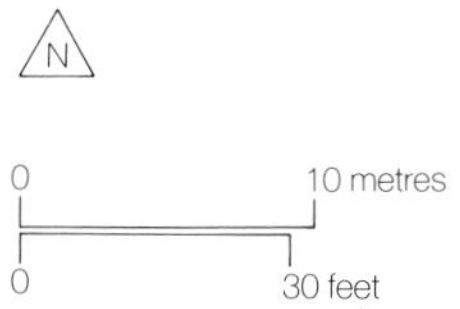

2

1

2

7

6

3

4

2

2

1

3

5

6

N

0   10 metres

0   30 feet

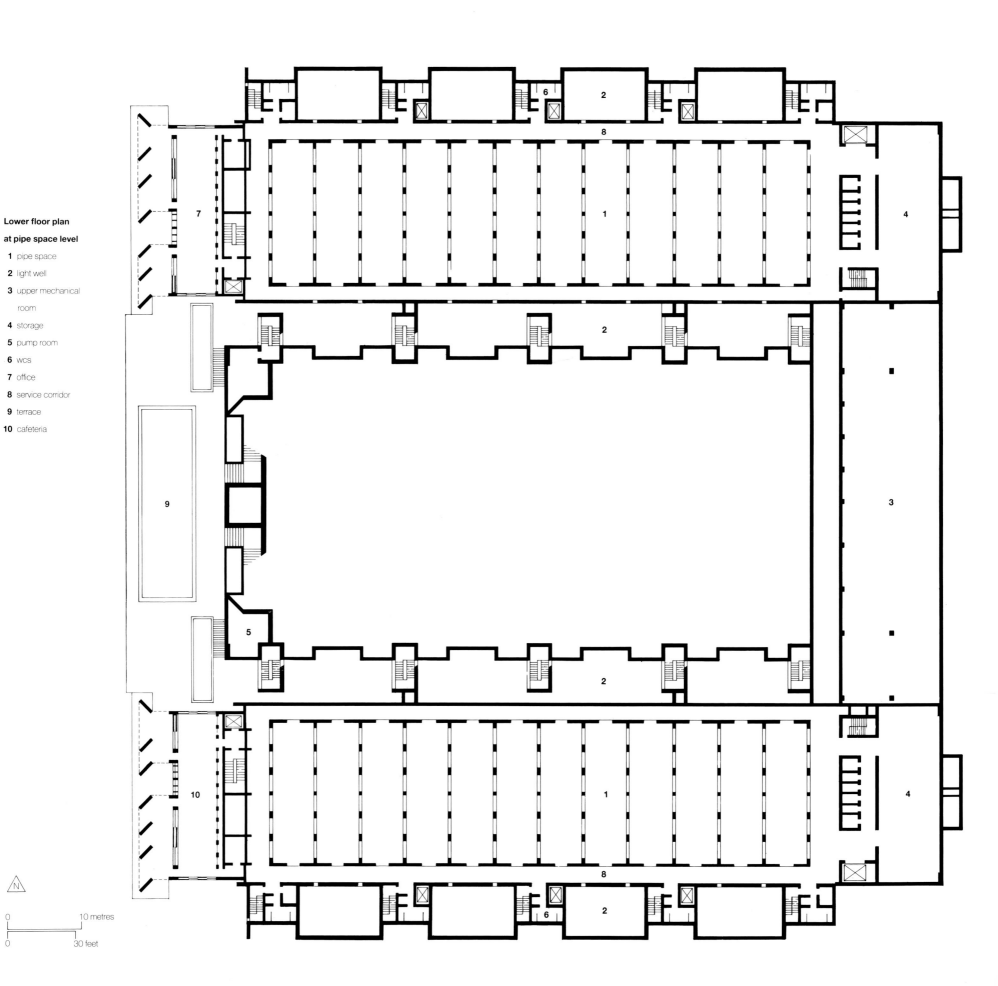

Lower floor plan
at pipe space level

1 pipe space
2 light well
3 upper mechanical
   room
4 storage
5 pump room
6 wcs
7 office
8 service corridor
9 terrace
10 cafeteria

0   10 metres
0   30 feet

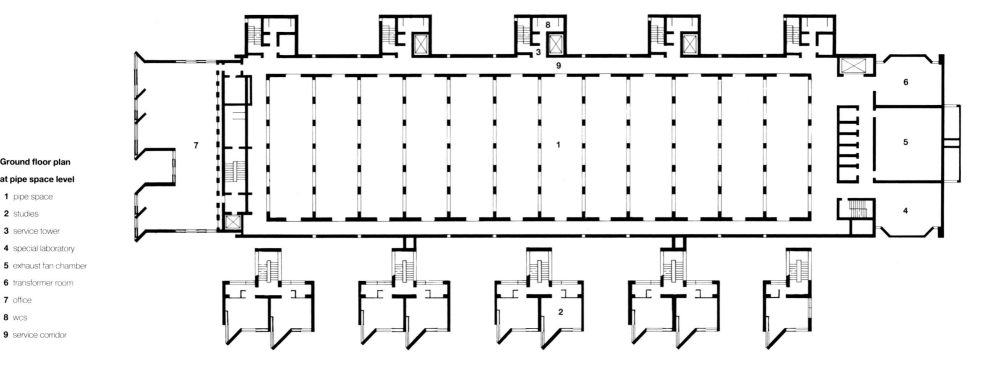

Ground floor plan
at pipe space level

1 pipe space
2 studies
3 service tower
4 special laboratory
5 exhaust fan chamber
6 transformer room
7 office
8 wcs
9 service corridor

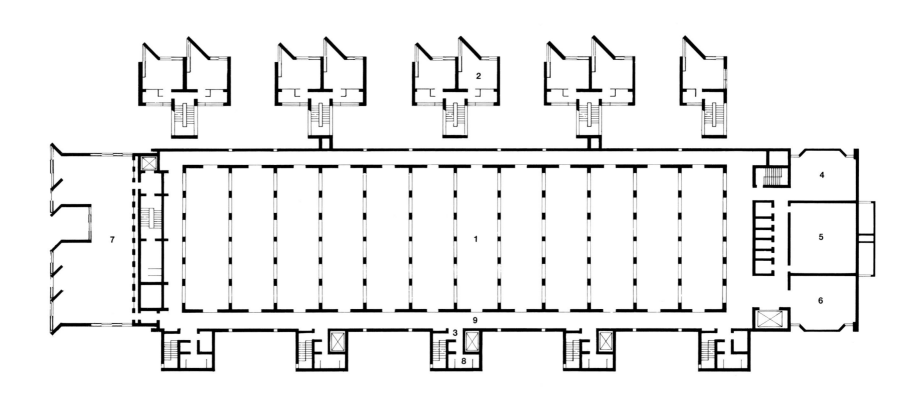

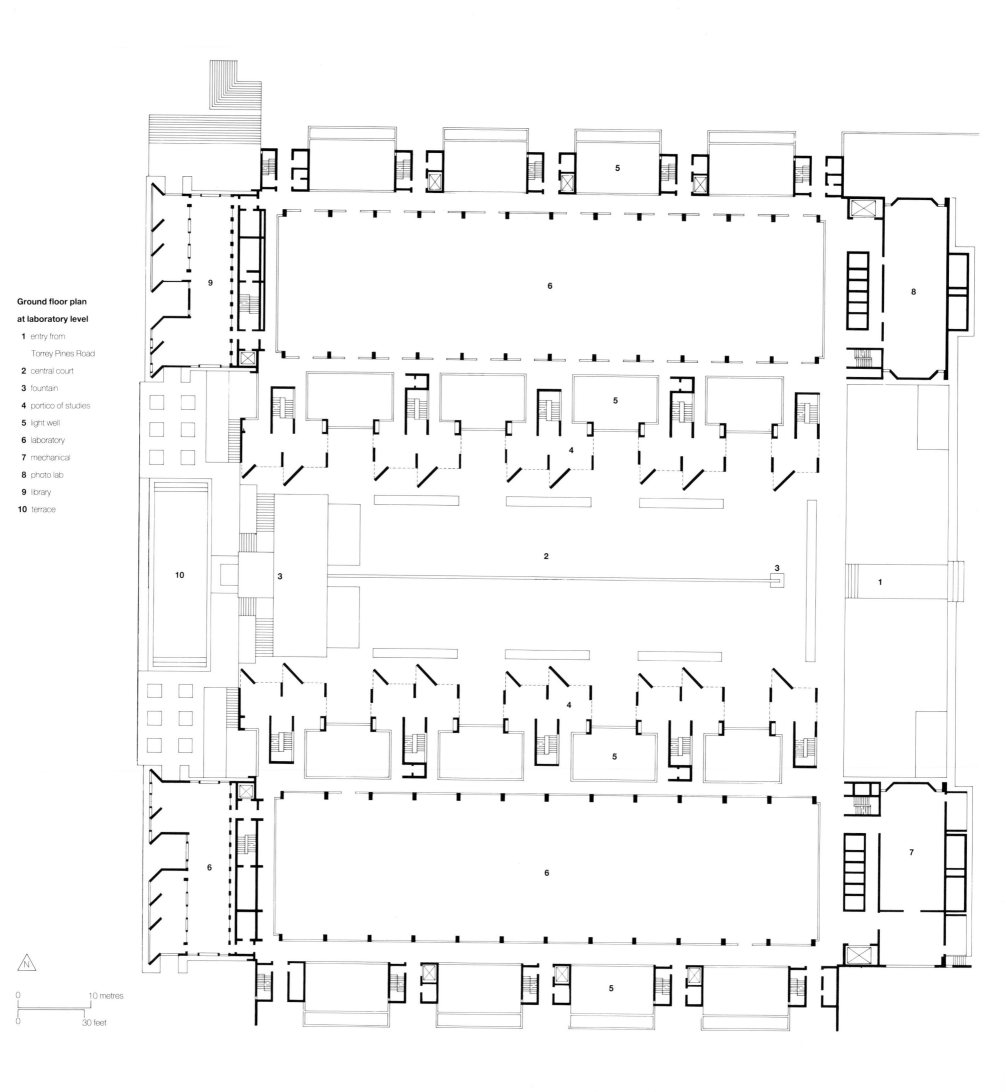

**Ground floor plan
at laboratory level**

1 entry from
  Torrey Pines Road
2 central court
3 fountain
4 portico of studies
5 light well
6 laboratory
7 mechanical
8 photo lab
9 library
10 terrace

0 ____ 10 metres
0 ____ 30 feet

Courtyard

paving plan

1 entry stair from
  Torrey Pines Road
2 fountain
3 water line
4 travertine pavers
5 portico of studies
6 light well
7 stairs to laboratories
8 terrace overlooking
  the Pacific

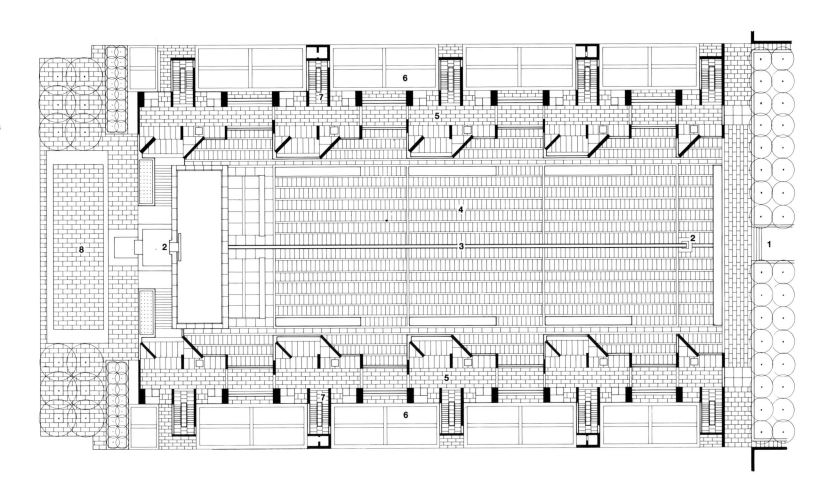

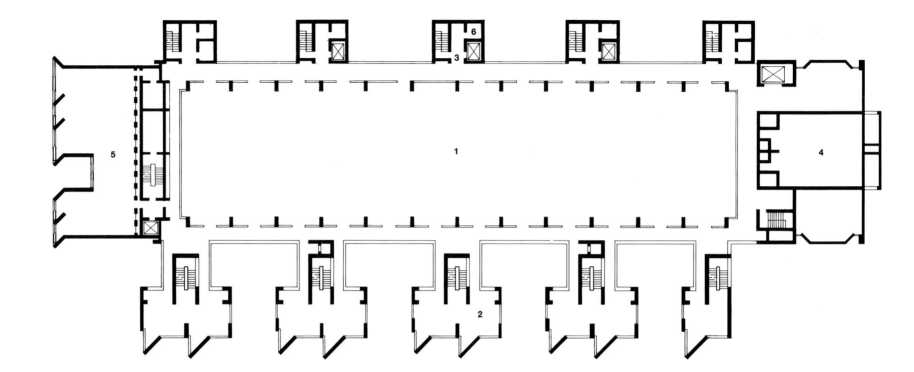

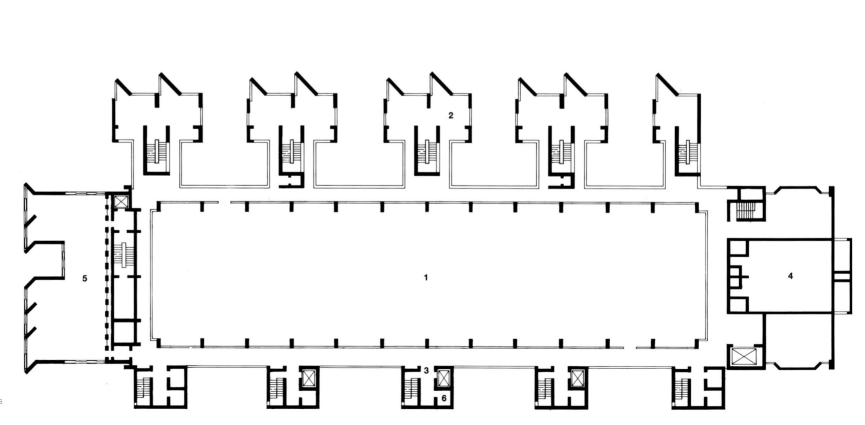

Upper floor plan

at laboratory level

1 laboratory

2 portico of studies

3 service tower

4 mechanical wing

5 office

6 wcs

0   10 metres

0   30 feet

Upper floor plan
at pipe space level

1 pipe space
2 studies
3 service tower
4 cooling tower
5 office
6 wcs
7 service corridor

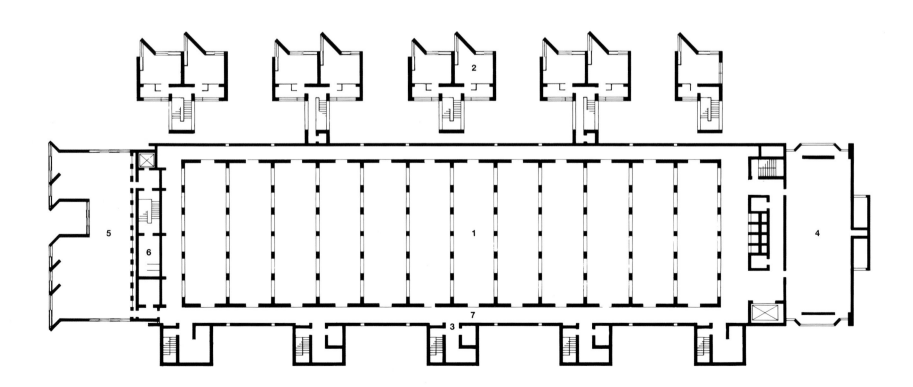

Section through
laboratories and
central court

1 central court

2 portico of studies

3 bridge to laboratories

4 light well

5 laboratory

6 interstitial mechanical
   space

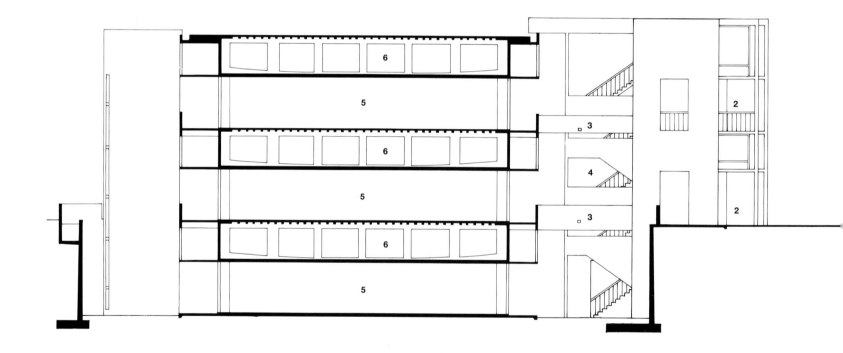

0   5 metres

0   15 feet

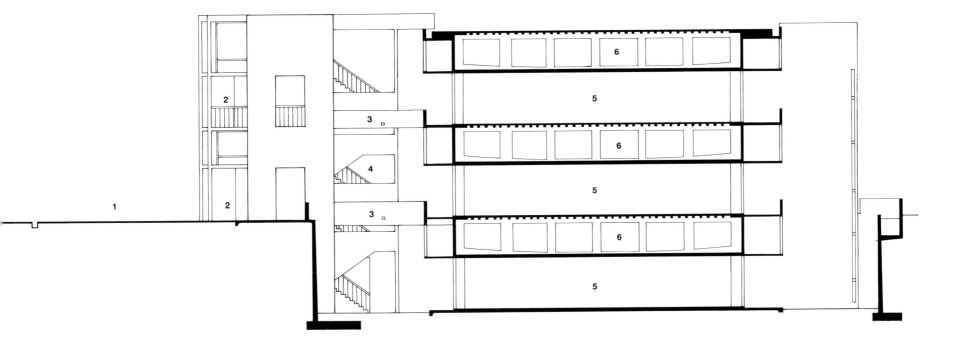

Section through
north office wing

1 entrance portico

2 office

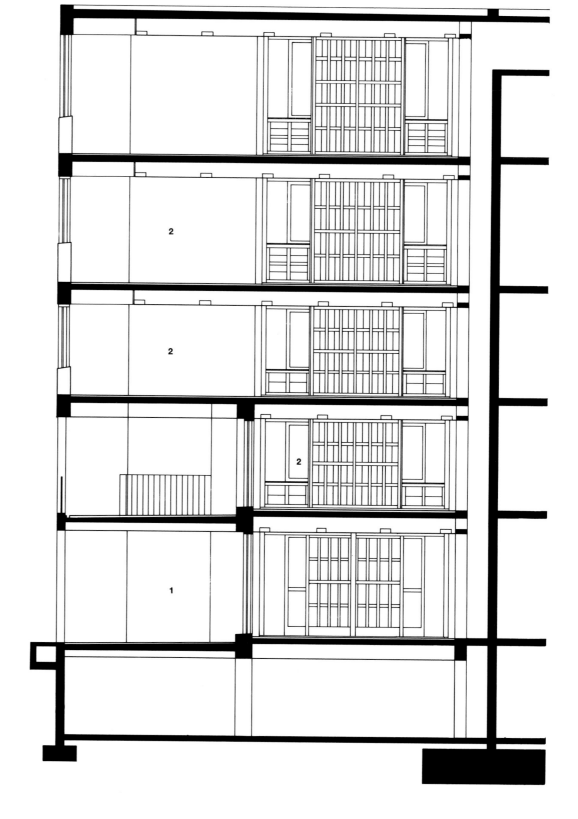

0 ⊢──────┤ 3 metres

0 ⊢──────┤ 10 feet

Probative detail
section through
sliding teak shutters
in a typical study

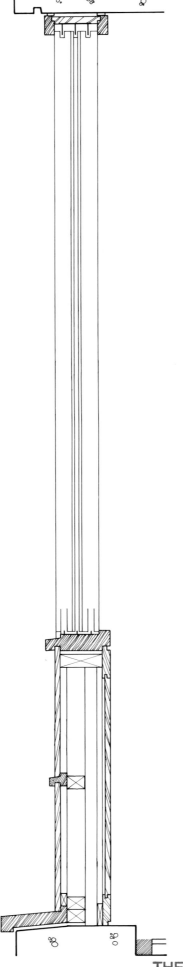

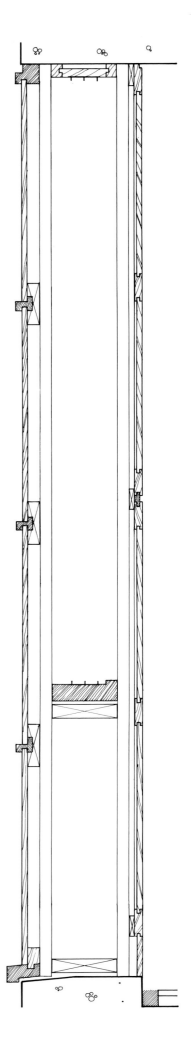

0 ————— 200mm

0 ————— 6 inches

**THE LIBRARY
TOWER HAMLETS COLLEGE
POPLAR HIGH STREET
LONDON E14 0AF
Tel: 0207 510 7763**

TWENTIETH-CENTURY CLASSICS

Beth Dunlop is the former architecture critic of the *Miami Herald* and currently writes on architecture for a variety of publications.
Denis Hector is an associate professor at the University of Miami School of Architecture where he is also Director of graduate programmes.

Walter Gropius
Bauhaus, Dessau

Dennis Sharp is a distinguished writer and scholar and has his own architectural practice in London. He is currently an RIBA Vice President, Director of the International Committee of Architectural Critics and Chairman of DOCOMOMO-UK. He has lectured at various institutions, including the Architectural Association in London, the Smithsonian Institute in Washington and Columbia University. He writes regularly for *Building Design* and *A+U*, was Editor of the *AA Quarterly* and *World of Architecture* and has written and edited several publications including *Twentieth Century Architecture; A Visual History* (1990) and *The Rationalists: Theory in the Modern Movement* (1978).

Acknowledgements Considerable help has been provided by working members of the Bauhaus in the preparation of this text and the author would like to thank Wolfgang Thöner, Bauhaus Research Fellow, and Frau Louise Schier at Dessau for their interest in the project and for supplying archival material. Sincere thanks also go to Jasper Hermann for his help at the old Weimar Bauhaus and David Blake of Messrs Crittalls for information on steel window systems; to Nancy Jackson for her patient retyping of the many drafts of the text and to the author's wife, the architect Yasmin Shariff, for her critical advice and transference of the text into a more workable format. Illustrations were provided by: Hochschule für Architektur und Bauwesen, Weimar (4); Dennis Sharp (5, 7, 26); Bookart Architecture Picture Library (6, 24, 25, 39); Reinhardt Friedrich* (15); Lucia Moholy* (34) and Walter Peterhaus* (37). *Bauhaus-Archiv, Berlin.

Le Corbusier
Unité d'Habitation

David Jenkins qualified at the Kingston Polytechnic School of Architecture and has worked variously with Ahrends Burton and Koralek, Terry Farrell & Company and James Stirling, Michael Wilford and Associates. He was Buildings Editor of the *Architects' Journal* and a commissioning editor at Phaidon Press. He is currently employed at Foster Associates.

Acknowledgements The author is grateful to the Fondation Le Corbusier for permission to reproduce sketches and drawings by Le Corbusier that are still in copyright, to Andrew Meade for his help with picture research, to Trevor Garnham for generously reading the manuscript and to Sandy Boyle in whose house this book was begun. Text illustrations were provided by the Architectural Press (1, 5, 7, 8, 10, 14–16, 30, 36, 41–45 and 48–51) and Lucien Hervé (27).

Louis I. Kahn
Salk Institute

James Steele has taught and practiced architecture in Philadelphia and in Saudi Arabia. He has been guest lecturer at Texas Tech University, writes frequently for the *Architectural Review* and *Architectural Design* magazines, and is currently Visiting Professor at the University of Southern California in Los Angeles. He is an important contributor to the Architecture in Detail series and author of *Los Angeles Architecture*, also published by Phaidon.

Acknowledgements The author acknowledges the role of Dr Jonas Salk who provided important information which was necessary in the preparation of this monograph, as well as that of Dianne D. Carter of the public relations department, and James Cox of the photography department of the Salk Institute. Dr Julia Moore Converse at the Louis I. Kahn Collection, The Architectural Archives, at the University of Pennsylvania also provided kind assistance in making drawings available, to be included here
with redrawing carried out by Ann Knudsen. He also expresses gratitude to Victoria Turkel, at the University of Southern California, who researched various aspects of the project. Illustrations were provided by Grant Mudford (1); Louis I. Kahn Collection, University of Pennsylvania and Pennsylvania Historical and Museum Commission copyright 1977 (6, 7, 14, 16, 17, 18, 19, 24 and 28); Ann Knudsen (8, 15) and Kazi Khaleed Ashraf (49).

Phaidon Press Limited
Regent's Wharf
All Saints Street
London N1 9PA

Twentieth-Century Classics first
published 1999
© 1999 Phaidon Press Limited
ISBN 0 7148 3868 3

A CIP catalogue record for this book is available
from the British Library.

Printed in Hong Kong

Bauhaus, Dessau originally published in
Architecture in Detail series 1993
© 1993 Phaidon Press Limited
Photography © 1993 Dennis Gilbert
Unité d'Habitation originally published in
Architecture in Detail series 1993
© 1993 Phaidon Press Limited
Photography © 1993 Peter Cook
Salk Institute originally published in
Architecture in Detail series 1993
© 1993 Phaidon Press Limited
Photography © 1993 Peter Aprahamian
unless otherwise stated